KRISHNA IN THE SKY
WITH DIAMONDS

The Bhagavad Gita
as Psychedelic Guide

SCOTT TEITSWORTH

Park Street Press
Rochester, Vermont • Toronto, Canada

Park Street Press
One Park Street
Rochester, Vermont 05767
www.ParkStPress.com

Text stock is SFI certified

Park Street Press is a division of Inner Traditions International

Library of Congress Cataloging-in-Publication Data
Teitsworth, Scott.
  Krishna in the sky with diamonds : the Bhagavad Gita as psychedelic guide /
Scott Teitsworth.
    p. cm.
  Includes bibliographical references (p.   ) and index.
  ISBN 978-1-59477-441-6 (pbk.) — ISBN 978-1-59477-711-0 (e-book)
  1. Bhagavadgita—Criticism, interpretation, etc. 2. Hallucinogenic drugs and
religious experience. I. Title.
  BL1138.66.T39 2012

                                                                    2011042241

Printed and bound in the United States by Lake Book Manufacturing
The text stock is SFI certified. The Sustainable Forestry Initiative® program
promotes sustainable forest management.

10   9   8   7   6   5   4   3   2   1

Text design and layout by Virginia Scott Bowman
This book was typeset in Garamond Premier Pro with Trajan and Copperplate
used as display typefaces

To send correspondence to the author of this book, mail a first-class letter to the
author c/o Inner Traditions • Bear & Company, One Park Street, Rochester, VT
05767, and we will forward the communication.

*In gratitude to Guru Nitya Chaitanya Yati, superb
teacher of the Bhagavad Gita, lifelong friend,
and continuing inspiration*

CONTENTS

PART 1

—·—

THE UNADORNED TEXT OF
CHAPTER XI OF THE BHAGAVAD GITA

PART 2

—·—

COMMENTARY ON CHAPTER XI:
THE UNITIVE VISION OF THE ABSOLUTE
(VIŚVARŪPA DARŚANA YOGA)

PROLOGUE

At the outset of the Bhagavad Gita, a man named Arjuna finds himself on the verge of a supremely challenging battle involving everything he holds dear. No matter who wins, he can foresee only madness and destruction as the outcome. His instinct, even though he is a famous warrior, is to turn and flee. He doesn't even want to think about it any more. But his chariot driver, Krishna, insists that he stand his ground. He tells him, "You only want to run away because you don't understand this situation and your place in it. Stay here with me and I will teach you."

Certain he is trapped in a situation with only disastrous options, Arjuna agrees, and the two enter a deep dialogue. They sit right in the middle of the battlefield, with swords clashing and arrows whizzing all around them. It is very important that they can have this seemingly impossible conversation without any need for protection. It tells us in pictorial language that the Gita's teaching is focused on how to live in this world, right in the thick of things, and is not about finding a better life somewhere else. In the final analysis there is nowhere to hide, nowhere to escape to.

After a lengthy instruction, Arjuna's fears are calmed and his intelligence is satisfied. All his questions and doubts have been resolved. Yet he has one more request. "Dear Krishna, it all makes sense to me now, and I appreciate that very much. But I would like to have a direct experience of what you have described to me.

Intellectual understanding is wonderful, but I need to feel it in my heart too. In my very bones. Is there some way for me to know this truth more intimately?"

Krishna answers, "Yes, certainly. I'm glad you asked." He mixes a special decoction known as soma, brewed from herbs and mushrooms, and in a sacred ceremony with a longstanding tradition he serves it to his disciple.

The soma he drinks blows Arjuna's mind wide open, revealing the underlying oneness of all existence to him. The impact is searingly direct and undeniable. It is as though a level of reality Arjuna had utterly forgotten was at last restored.

No matter how fine a teaching might be, it is only words and their associated concepts until it is converted by the learner into a direct experience. Chemists study up-to-date theories about the elements and their properties, but they don't become true chemists until they handle actual chemicals and start mixing them together. Before that they are merely students. Teachers first learn the principles of teaching in school, but they are only in training until they go out and stand up in front of a classroom. This is a common progression for nearly all expressions of *dharma,* a person's true calling, including in spiritual matters. The time has come in Arjuna's unfoldment to move from theory to practice, to put his knowledge into action via realization—in other words, to make the wisdom he has imbibed real. The soma ceremony impels him to do just that.

The inner nature Arjuna discovers is our inner nature, too. It is charged with intense joy and energy, but we have lost touch with it. Abstractly believing that we are an integral part of a coherently inter-connected universe is well and good, but knowing it as a living reality sweeps away layer after layer of illusion, of false speculation. Soma peels back the veil our own minds have woven and restores us to harmony with our true being. There is no greater bliss on Earth.

One likely result of such an overwhelming experience is that we do not have any way to comprehend it, to wrap our minds around it. What we face transcends our definitions, no matter how bountiful those might be. But to live a viable life as an embodied being we need to integrate this new awareness into our knowledge base. Krishna will spend the rest of the Gita—seven more complete chapters—helping Arjuna to do just that. When his integration is finally accomplished, Krishna lets him know that he has become a truly independent soul, capable of making his own expert decisions. He no longer needs to be subservient to any person, system, or idea. He is free.

INTRODUCTION

The Bhagavad Gita is one of the most important of the ancient writings of the human race. It forms part of the Mahabharata, probably the world's longest epic, which gleans the cream of the wisdom of a large and disparate group of thinkers in what is today northern India. Of uncertain date, the earliest changeover from oral to written form is likely to have been roughly contemporary with the Buddha, around 500 BCE. Chapter XI of the Bhagavad Gita, titled "Viśvarūpa Darśana Yoga" or "The Unitive Vision of the Absolute," is one of the most eloquent descriptions of a complex psychedelic experience ever recorded. The present book is intended to decode its archaic language and symbolism to clarify the helpful intentions of its anonymous author, known only as Vyasa (Writer).

In the Gita, as it is affectionately called, there are just two main characters—the seeker Arjuna and his guru Krishna—plus a narrator, Sanjaya. Krishna is a human being, but in the reverential attitude of India a guru is also a living incarnation of the Absolute, the supreme principle, that which leaves nothing out. In Vedanta, the philosophical system of the Gita and its close cousins the Upanishads, everyone and all things are the Absolute in essence, and the seeker's path, such as it is, is to come to know this truth. It is a path that begins and ends right where you are.

Arjuna and Krishna are talking on the battlefield in the middle of a great war. Some people are bothered that the Gita unfolds in such a discordant environment, imagining that a scripture should be set in a garden of paradise. But life is filled with conflicts, great and small. The Gita's message is that we are sure to face difficulties throughout our life, but we can learn to manage them well. It is not about how to avoid problems by making an escape or by holding on to a single predetermined viewpoint.

The setting of the battlefield also tells us that the way to peace is not through rearranging the outside world. The world, with its complex problems, will almost certainly not be fixed by us no matter how hard we try. But we are eminently capable of major improvements to ourselves, especially given some expert guidance. Life is a struggle and a fight much of the time, and no one has ever succeeded in taming it for long. We need to find solid ground within ourselves, so that whether the winds blow fair or foul we will not be knocked over. Paradoxically, once we heal ourselves and become stabilized we can begin to have a beneficial impact on our surroundings, but if we confront the world's ills from a discordant position, our efforts will be plagued with unintended and often tragic consequences.

SOMA

The Bhagavad Gita presents a detailed scientific psychology lightly clothed in the type of religious-sounding narrative in favor at the time. Being a textbook on what is required to produce a truly liberated adult human being, it does not impose any rigid structure or set of rules to follow. Its goal is to teach people how to make their own decisions based on their deepest nature, because, while that nature is constant and dependable, circumstances are forever in flux. What is appropriate in one instance may be a deadly mistake in another. A truly awake human being will know how to act well without having to seek direction from any scripture or law library.

As in the era when the Gita was composed, the preceding Vedic age was a period of intense religious ferment and exploration. The writings that have been preserved from it, the Vedas, record the poetic fancies and psychological insights garnered by seekers of truth over a long period of time. The Bhagavad Gita and other contemporary writings were written to highlight the best ideas of the Vedas while discarding their excess baggage. They also added new insights, the most important being monotheism in the sense of recognizing the overarching unity of life.

The Vedas are replete with references to the ritual use of a substance called *soma* for religious inspiration. The soma ceremony, in which the potion was imbibed, was a frequent practice in ancient India, and it infuses the Vedic scriptures to a remarkable degree. The formula for its preparation is unknown, but it is thought to have included psychedelic mushrooms. As we will see from the record presented here, soma's effects are quite similar, if not identical, to the psychedelics we know of today, particularly psilocybin and LSD.

Although the later philosophic critiques of the Upanishads and the Bhagavad Gita tend to be rationally oriented, ecstasy remains as an important feature. *Gita* means "song," and enlightenment lifts the heart like a song. A song differs from ordinary speech in the same way that ecstasy differs from ordinary life. The Gita's teaching is designed to convert the individual notes of knowledge we are composed of into an enchanting musical symphony.

We don't know why the formula for soma was lost over the passage of many years, but changing attitudes may have redirected the exploration of the mind to other, more ascetic practices. With the sacred soma ceremonies forgotten, what they had once accomplished began to be viewed solely as a mystical transmission from guru to disciple, brought about by a certain touch or ritual, or simply some secret knowledge. Today this is the firmly established orthodox position, but when the Gita was written there was no doubt that what brought about realization was the ingestion of soma. Mental preparation was important, even crucial, but only in rare cases was it enough to ignite realization. With the assistance of the soma medicine, however, any properly prepared disciple could have a mind-expanding experience.

Fasting, wandering in the desert, meditation, extreme exercise, near-death experiences, and many more techniques can produce profound mental and emotional states, and all have been practiced by humans since ancient times. However, there is every reason to believe that the events described in this chapter are a psychedelic medicine trip. Nothing is explicitly stated, but the resemblance is striking for anyone who has undertaken one. There is an archetypal opening-up process being described here that can tell us a great deal about how the mind responds spiritually to a variety of intense stimulations. While sometimes harrowing enough to be severely unpleasant, a carefully planned and guided soma trip is comparatively civilized and much less hazardous than most of the alternatives.

Modern orthodox sensibilities have overlaid a puritanical blanket of denial onto the innocence and sacredness of the ancient soma rituals. Only in the second half of the twentieth century did those ceremonies come to be appreciated anew as having tremendous spiritual potential. Now that they have, they demand a place in a fully realized commentary.

PROPER PREPARATION

As far as we know, the Bhagavad Gita has become a highly revered scripture only in relatively recent times. In keeping with the world-wide historical trend toward puritanism in religion, the drug element implied in it, which is limited to this single chapter, has been replaced with a belief in a purely inspirational experience such as can be achieved through yoga or meditation. While this is a healthy development in some respects, psychedelic medicines have the capacity to confer the equivalent of many years of strenuous practice or therapy in a much shorter period of time and without pushing the body to the edge of death, as occurs with fasting, dehydration, solitary confinement, and similar techniques. In the modern era, the use of psychedelics has been aggressively suppressed, but they are beginning to find their rightful place in a sane but cautious pharmacopeia once again.

Psychedelics contribute to a long list of positive mental attitudes, aiding in internal adjustments that foster happiness and expanded intelligence, while promoting outwardly directed values such as tolerance, humility, loving kindness, compassion, and so on. In the Gita, the pupil Arjuna, guided by his guru Krishna, uses soma to help him make his theoretical training real. The first ten chapters detail his lengthy course of mental preparation. Chapter XI deals with his psychedelic sojourn in which he converts the theories he has been taught into direct experience, and the remaining seven chapters show him how to integrate his experience into a viable way of life.

Very few people who have taken psychedelic medicines in the last fifty years have undergone the extensive preparation that was once considered a prerequisite, as evidenced by Arjuna's regimen. Even fewer have had the opportunity to be guided back into a dynamic life-expression by such a compassionate helpmate as Krishna. It is to fill this important vacuum that the present interpretation is offered. For those interested in the complete psychology, the entire Gita is interpreted from a modern standpoint in my online commentary called Nitya Teachings.[1]

The Gita does not explicitly recommend any specific form of ritual behavior, but it provides intelligent guidelines for bringing each life to its full potential. The way taken will depend on individual choice and the so-called accidents of fate. Because of my own familiarity with psychedelic medicines, especially LSD, I feel qualified to describe their spiritual efficacy in broad outline. The Gita's illuminating perspective on Arjuna's visionary experience, whatever it might have been, could well serve as a blueprint for anyone in a position to safely attempt a comparable experiment.

OVERCOMING RESISTANCE

The long-standing hostility of mainstream society to psychedelic medicines is well known. Scriptures like the Gita have shared in that acrimoniousness to some degree by having their message diluted and even inverted. Where the original idea is to promote human unity with the cosmos, scriptures are often interpreted to exalt certain individuals and reinforce the widespread conviction that liberation is only for one single rare and exceptional person who lived in the distant past. That means there is no possibility of freedom for the rest of us without divine intervention on our behalf, or the miraculous return of that special person. The Gita is frequently cited to promulgate Krishna in such a role, and doing so totally undermines its most important tenet: that the Absolute is inherent in everyone and accessible to all who seek it.

The central claim of Vedantic philosophy, as presented in the Bhagavad Gita and the Upanishads, is that each person is the Absolute in essence, and our challenge is to come to remember that truth in a world where objects and events constantly distract us from it, often even intentionally. This not only gives us unlimited hope, it empowers us to do our best. We are accorded the highest respect imaginable in advance. If everyone and everything is sacred, then there is no possibility of sacrilege. We have no need for divine intervention, because we are already miraculous. Life is a continuous "divine intervention," so what more could be needed?

The marginalizing of psychedelic drugs by a paranoiac power elite is no accident. Like the Gita, psychedelics impart revolutionary insight in its truest sense. The realization that all humans, indeed all entities comprised of atoms, are essentially one, and that our nature is therefore equally "divine," instantly puts the lie to the attitudes of the vested interests that benefit from our world being structured on the basis of masters and slaves, chosen and cursed. The falsity of beliefs that elevate one small group and denigrate the rest is immediately obvious to a mind expanded by psychedelic medicine.

Along the same lines, author Barbara Kingsolver asks rhetorically, in her recent book *The Lacuna,* "Does a man become a revolutionary out of the belief he's entitled to joy rather than submission?"[2] Nothing could be more central to our happiness than this type of conversion.

An important part of the revolutionary nature of psychedelic substances is that they encourage nonviolence. Their action resembles a rising tide gently melting sand castles on the beach, dissolving temporary structures that loom large while the tide is out. By contrast, the sand castles of an elite can only be defended with overt and covert coercion, so their position depends on inducing violent opposition and then smashing it. If one side can discover how not to be drawn into violent reaction to the other, the game will come to an end. Thus there is no greater threat to the status quo than realization.

The special technique of the Gita is to unify all polarizations, inwardly and outwardly, in what is called *yoga*. If we stop feeding the differences, they will melt away. The way to achieve this is to become fully realized human beings. No external goal, and certainly no aggressive action, can bring it about. The temptation to engage in partisan battle can only be resisted with an inner calm founded on wisdom.

Timothy Leary's exhortation to "Turn on, Tune in, and Drop out" should be understood in this light. "Turn on," of course, means to take LSD or another psychedelic. "Tune in" is to rediscover your true nature as an enlightened and joyous spirit being. "Drop out" doesn't mean drop out of life. Quite the contrary, it invites us to abandon the death trip of submission to authority and remain tuned in to our full potential. We should drop out of all the things that prevent us from tuning in. The revolutionary nature of Leary's phrase echoes the call of the Gita from the ancient past. We must not make the common mistake of treating dropping out as the most important part. "Turn on" and "Drop out" are the thesis and antithesis; "Tune in" is the synthesis, the main course. Tuning in to what we really are is the key to a life worth living, one that substitutes joy for submission.

Scientists are constrained to limit themselves to a search based on facts, strictly from the outside looking in, but philosophers, and particularly yogis—dedicated seekers of truth—are free to employ an inside out approach also. The ideal is for both orientations to mutually reinforce and correct each other. Obviously, psychedelics instruct from the inside out. Afterward, balancing their influence requires tempering with some careful "outside in" analysis.

Despite the postulation of an Absolute, which keeps consciousness properly oriented and is common to all systems, whether philosophical, religious, or scientific, there is no such thing as absolute realization. Anything realized has to be relative, less than the whole, which means there is no absolute right or wrong, nor any last word. Whenever the mind goes beyond its accustomed boundaries, it undergoes an expansion that feels like liberation or realization, but no one has yet ascertained any end to human potential. Greater expansion is a perennial possibility.

Because of this, there is always more to be discovered. Once we realize that our knowledge is inevitably partial, we will know that learning never ends and there is no ultimate panacea. Anyone claiming finalized answers is in fact seriously deluded and is very likely intending to manipulate others for personal benefit. In any case the idea of finality brings growth to a halt. Psychedelics convincingly drive this truth home by flinging the doors of perception wide open.

In the aftermath of an intense psychedelic experience like Arjuna's, there is a period of profound openness and vulnerability to suggestions. Arjuna is fortunate to be under the guidance of a wide-awake and compassionate guru who will carefully ease him back into the flow of everyday life. After the brief period of legal psychedelics in the mid-twentieth century came to an end, many who experimented with them were unsupervised and unprepared. They encountered all sorts of bizarre and negative influences during the critical recovery period, eventually including intentional sabotage by governmental agents provocateurs, and some serious damage occurred. Even a seemingly simple act like watching television can lodge twisted attitudes deep in the psyche, which continue to cause confusion for a very long time afterward. The wake of a trip, like early childhood, is a time for great care in nurturing only the best aspects of life, because what is encountered goes much deeper than usual and is very hard to dislodge. The Gita's attitude is clear: only take these medicines in the right circumstances, with proper preparation, and under the guidance of a loving person you trust and who knows you well.

In a way, this part of the Gita makes more sense as an instruction manual for the guides, rather than for the ones taking the soma. The presentation is rather frightening for a prospective tripper, but it prepares the guide for some touchy situations that may well occur. And of course it has a great deal to offer those with no interest at all in psychedelic excursions.

THE PRESENT COMMENTATOR

I had the good fortune to study the Gita with an exceptionally intelligent and broad-minded guru, Nitya Chaitanya Yati, who taught it almost continuously to enthusiastic audiences in Portland, Oregon, from 1970 to 1976. After that I worked with him to prepare the typescript of his own Gita commentary, and since then I have had numerous occasions to teach the work myself.

Due to my dissatisfaction with aspects of a number of the better-known commentaries, which among other things universally downplay soma, I began compiling a detailed version of my own thoughts, working through the Gita verse by verse. As I contemplated chapter XI, a nagging suspicion that it really was about soma experience grew into a certainty with verse 6, where the "demigods" mentioned symbolize important stages of a trip. Because of strikingly similar experiences I had had many years before, that part of my commentary blossomed into the small book you hold in your hands. The first part of the book presents the unadorned text, while the second part adds a detailed commentary for each of the verses. Sanskrit is such an allusive language that a vast amount of information is transmitted in a very few words. My comments are examples of the kind of meditative expansion that any student of the Gita is expected to make as they study the work, fleshing out the bare bones with resonant insights.

My guru's teacher, Nataraja Guru, electrified the world of Gita commentary with his own scientifically minded interpretation in 1961, and his book has been continuously in print in India ever since. His translation, which is the one used here, replaces the typical religious attitude with a more scientific and philosophical one. Neither of us employs what Nataraja Guru called "Lord Lordism," the displacement of the meaning of life to a remote and superior god, which is nearly universal in Gita commentaries while being foreign to the spirit of the Gita itself.

The majority of commentaries refer to Krishna as Lord or God, but those of my lineage prefer the more philosophical term *Absolute*. The Absolute is all-inclusive: there is nothing that is not it. If you think something isn't the Absolute, then your idea of absoluteness is flawed.

Obviously Lord and God are more specific and limited terms, calling to mind a gap between them or it and us. With Krishna, they make us think of a blue-skinned, flute-wielding playboy rather than an all-pervasive principle.

The Absolute is more an ideal than a fact, and therefore it is not accessible directly through any accumulation of knowledge. As ideas are refined, they can approach the Absolute ever more closely from the outside, but there is always a gap, most beautifully depicted in Michelangelo's painting *The Creation of Adam,* where an anthropomorphized Absolute and a primordial human reach toward each other in a cosmic gesture, fingers nearly but not quite touching.

Many techniques can be successful at causing a spark to jump the gap, and the smaller the gap the easier it becomes. Intelligent understanding brings the sides closer together. When a seeker and the object of their speculative approach are finally sparked into direct contact, it is known as union with the Absolute. In everyone's life there is plenty of scope for action—good, bad, or indifferent—but what makes it fully realized and particularly valuable is some type of direct experience of the Absolute itself. As we will see, the impact of such an experience is profound, infusing and informing every aspect of existence with a dramatically heightened awareness.

Like the Absolute, the guru is a principle rather than an actual human being. *Guru* means whatever removes the darkness of our ignorance. *Bhagavan* is commonly translated as "Lord," but here it is used to indicate Krishna as a guru representing the Absolute. The word *bhagavan* means "radiance" or "glory," the Light from which all things manifest. The historical trend of religion is to start with a vision of pure light, but as it fades over time into a concept instead of a direct experience, the light becomes personified as a god before which everyone should bow. We are aiming to return to the firsthand version here, in which *bhagavan* is not used as a term expressing abject devotion to a god. It is indicative of respect and admiration toward an excellent teacher, which is the correct attitude to have toward a guru.

Nataraja Guru visualized the eighteen chapters of the Gita as forming an arch shape, with the first and last chapters resting on the solid ground of everyday life, which he called the horizontal plane, and the two middle chapters, IX and X, forming the keystone and dealing only with the most sublime or vertical aspects of the Absolute. In between are graded series linking the two poles of the horizontal and vertical, the everyday and the spiritual. Chapter XI is the first reentry of the seeker Arjuna after the transcendental, fully vertical portion, where his mind is lifted as high as it can go. This chapter is somewhat anomalous with the rest of the Gita, and it can more easily stand on its own than any of the others.

We might expect Arjuna's mind-blowing vision of the nature of the Absolute to come at the high point of the arch of the Gita, in chapters IX or X. In fact, Arjuna's experience takes place a little past the peak. The reason for this is that the two central chapters are focused almost exclusively on Krishna's nature as the Absolute. In their purely vertical orientation, there is not yet enough of Arjuna present to have any kind of experience, no matter how sublime. Krishna's glowing description of the Absolute in those two chapters did clarify his mind, though, and now he is properly prepared for a brief but vital merger with the fundamental ground of existence.

The Gita is one of the most commented-upon books of all time, and it would seem its subject matter should have long been exhausted. But that is by no means the case, and my version is unique in many ways. In particular, chapter XI has not to my knowledge been interpreted in terms of a soma experience. Because of humanity's pressing need to find noncoercive methods to ameliorate its violent and destructive tendencies, this aspect of the ancient knowledge has a special value. How to use powerful mind-altering agents wisely being more attractive to many people than wading through an entire discipline of understanding the universe, that is the main focus here. I am not dismayed, because the one undoubtedly leads to the other. Psychedelics are indeed "gateway drugs" in that they are very likely to lead to an indulgence in stronger stuff: open exploration of the mind and the meaning of life.

PART 1

The Unadorned Text of Chapter XI of the Bhagavad Gita

TRANSLATED BY NATARAJA GURU

1   Arjuna said:

By that speech which has been spoken by You out of favor for me—the highest secret known as pertaining to the Self—this, my confusion, has vanished.

2   The origin and dissolution of beings have also been heard by me in elaboration from You, O Krishna, as also Your unexpended greatness.

3   So it is as You have said Yourself, Supreme Lord; I desire to see Your divine Form, O Supreme Person.

4   If You think that it is possible for me to see it, then do You, O Master of Yoga, show me Your never-decreasing Self.

5   Krishna said:

Behold, Arjuna, My forms, by hundreds and thousands, various in kind, divine, and of varied colors and shapes.

6   Behold the Adityas, the Vasus, the Rudras, the two Asvins, and also the Maruts; behold many marvels never seen before.

7   Now behold here in My body the whole world, including the static and the dynamic, unitively established, and whatever else you desire to see.

8   But if you are unable to see Me with this your (human) eye, I give you a divine eye; behold My sovereign Yoga.

9   Sanjaya said:

Having thus spoken, then, O King, the great Master of Yoga showed Arjuna the supreme Godly Form.

10   With many faces and eyes, with many marvelous aspects, with many divine ornaments, with many divine weapons held aloft,

11   wearing divine garlands and vestures, anointed with divine perfumes and unguents, a God representing sheer marvel, without end, universally facing.

12   If the splendor of a thousand suns were to rise together

in the sky, that might resemble the splendor of that great Soul.

13 There Arjuna then beheld the whole world, divided into many kinds, unitively established in the body of the God of gods.

14 Then Arjuna, struck with amazement, with his hair standing on end, reverently bowing his head to the God, and with joined palms, spoke.

15 Arjuna said:
I see the gods, O God, in Your body, and all specific groups of beings, Brahma, the Lord, established on his lotus seat, and all seers and divine serpents.

16 I see You on every side, of boundless form, with multitudinous arms, stomachs, faces and eyes; neither Your end nor Your middle nor Your beginning do I see, O Lord of the Universe, O Universal Form!

17 I behold You with diadem, mace and discus, glowing everywhere as a mass of light, hard to look at, everywhere blazing like fire and sun, immeasurable.

18 You are the Imperishable, the Supreme that is to be known; You are the ultimate Basis of this universe; You are the unexpended and everlasting Custodian of (natural) law; You are the immemorial Person, I believe.

19 I see You without beginning, middle, or end, of never ending force, of numberless arms, having moon and sun for eyes, Your face like a lit fire of sacrifice burning this universe with Your own radiance.

20 The space between heaven, earth, and the intermediate realm is pervaded by You alone, as also the quarters; having seen this wonderful, terrible form of Yours, the three worlds are in distress, O Great Self.

21 Into You enter those hosts of the Suras, some in fear of You mutter with joined palms, bands of great rishis and

Perfected Ones hail You with the cry "May it be well!" and praise You with resounding hymns.

22 The Rudras, Adityas, Vasus and Sadhyas, Visvas and the two Asvins, Maruts and Ushmapas, hosts of Gandharvas, Yakshas, Asuras and Siddhas, all gaze at You, wonderstruck.

23 Seeing Your great form, with many faces and eyes, of many arms, thighs, and feet, with many stomachs, with many terrible teeth, the worlds are distressed, as also myself.

24 On seeing You touching the sky, shining in many a color, with mouths wide open, with large fiery eyes, my inmost self intensely distressed, I find neither courage nor control, O All-Pervading One.

25 Having seen Your mouths fearful with teeth, like time's devouring flames, I lose my spatial bearings and find no joy; be gracious, O Lord of gods, Container of the world!

26 All these sons of Dhritarastra, with hosts of rulers, Bhisma, Drona, and that son of a charioteer, with our warrior chiefs,

27 are rushing into Your fearful mouths, terrible with teeth; some are found sticking in the gaps between the teeth with their heads crushed to powder.

28 As many rushing torrents of rivers race toward the ocean, so do these heroes in the world of men enter Your flaming mouths.

29 As moths speed into a blazing fire to be destroyed, just so do these worlds also speed into Your mouths unto their destruction.

30 You lick up all worlds, devouring on every side with Your flaming mouths, filling the whole world with glory. Your fierce rays are blazing forth, O All-Pervading One.

31 Tell me who You are, so fierce in form! I bow to You, O
Superior God. Be gracious! I want to understand You,
O Primal One, nor do I know Your positive continued
becoming.

32 Krishna said:

I am world-destroying Time, grown into hardened
maturity, operating here continuously, desolating
the worlds. Even without you, none of the warriors
standing in the opposing armies shall continue to exist.

33 Therefore, arise and gain fame! Conquering your foes,
enjoy the realm of abundance. By Me they have already
been slain. Be the incidental cause only, Arjuna.

34 Drona and Bhishma, Jayadratha, Karna, and the other
great battle heroes, are all slain by Me. Do not be
distressed. Fight on, you shall conquer in battle your
rival co-warriors.

35 Sanjaya said:

Having heard that speech, Arjuna, stuttering emotionally
and trembling with fear, with palms joined
worshipfully, bowed down before Krishna and spoke
these words:

36 Arjuna said:

O Krishna, it is but right that the world is delighted in
praising You, that demons fly in fear to every quarter,
and that all hosts of perfected ones bow in adoration to
You.

37 And why should they not bow to You, O Great Self,
more venerable even than Brahma, the first maker, O
Endless God of gods, Basis of the Universe! You are
the Imperishable One, existence and nonexistence, and
what is beyond even that.

38 You are the First of the gods, and the Ancient Spirit;
You are the Supreme Basis of the Universe; You are
both the Knower and the Knowable; You are the

(transcendent) Beyond and the (immanent) Receptacle (here); the universe is pervaded by You, O One of Limitless Form!

39   You are the God of Wind, Death, Fire, Ocean, the Moon, first of Progenitors and the Great-Grandsire. Hail! Hail to You! A thousand times and again, hail! Hail to You!

40   Prostrations to You before and after; prostrations to You on every side; O All, of endless potency and immeasurable strength, You terminate all, then You become all!

41   Whatever I have said rashly, from carelessness or fondness, addressing You as "O Krishna, O Yadava, O Comrade," thinking of You as an intimate and ignorant of Your greatness,

42   and for whatever jesting irreverence I may have shown You, whether at play, reposing or seated, or at meals, either when remaining by myself or when You were present, that I ask you to forgive, O Unpredicable One!

43   You are the Father of the world, of the moving and unmoving; You are to be reverenced by this world, and are the Supreme Guru; none is Your equal; how then could there be one greater than You, even in the three worlds, O One of Incomparable Greatness!

44   Therefore bowing down and prostrating my body, I seek Your grace, O Adorable Lord; (it is but proper that) You should bear with me, as father to son, as friend to friend, as lover to beloved.

45   I am glad having seen what has never been seen by anyone before, and my mind is troubled with fear; O God, be pleased to show me that very form, O God of gods, O Abode of the Universe;

46   I want to see You even so, diademmed, with mace and

discus in Your hand; assume that very form with four arms, O Thousand-Armed, O One of Universal Form!

47 Krishna said:

By My favor, Arjuna, this supreme form has been shown, by union with the Self, made up of light, universal, endless, primal, never before seen by any other than yourself.

48 Neither by the Vedas, sacrifices, nor by study, nor by gifts, nor by ritual, nor by severe austerities, can I possibly be seen in such a form in the human world, by anyone other than you.

49 Be not distressed, do not be confused, having seen such a terrible form of Mine; free from fear, mentally comforted, again behold that very form of Mine (presently) here.

50 Sanjaya said:

Having thus spoken to Arjuna, Krishna again showed His own form, and the Great Self, becoming mild in form, consoled him who was terrified.

51 Arjuna said:

Beholding again this Your mild human form, I am now calm, with my mind restored to its natural state.

52 Krishna said:

This form of Mine which you have seen is very hard to see indeed; even the gods ever aspire to behold this form.

53 Not by worship, nor by austerity, nor by gifts, nor by sacrifice, can I be seen in this form as you have seen Me.

54 But by devotion that excludes all else I can be known, seen, and in principle entered into.

55 He who does actions that are Mine, whose Supreme is Myself, whose devotion is to Me, devoid of attachment, free from enmity to all beings—he reaches Me, Arjuna.

COMMENTARY ON CHAPTER XI

THE UNITIVE VISION OF THE ABSOLUTE (VIŚVARŪPA DARŚANA YOGA)

ARJUNA SAID:

BY THAT SPEECH WHICH HAS BEEN SPOKEN BY YOU OUT OF FAVOR FOR ME—THE HIGHEST SECRET KNOWN AS PERTAINING TO THE SELF—THIS, MY CONFUSION, HAS VANISHED.

This chapter of the Bhagavad Gita begins with Arjuna expressing his appreciation to Krishna that the Guru's words from the earlier chapters have removed his confusion about how to live his life. Very shortly he is going to ask for a direct experience of what he has learned, and in response Krishna will serve him a psychedelic beverage known as *soma* and act as a guide while his trip unfolds. The story of their journey together serves as the theme of our study.

Vedanta, the philosophical system that embraces the Gita, holds that words are the magical link that bridges the gap between the cosmic and the mundane, the transcendent and the immanent, ideals and actualities. Such matched pairs are viewed in yoga as the two sides or "poles" of a single coin that need to be understood in relation to each other. Neither pole can adequately stand on its own. Implicit in the Gita is the belief that guru and disciple comprise the central bipolarity—the gold coin—in the search for truth, and here Arjuna is acknowledging that his relationship to Krishna is ideal. When the bipolarity is perfect between the two sides of the "conversation," it opens the door to a cosmic vision of the Absolute, which is the key to unlocking many of life's problems.

Talk therapy has lost a measure of respect in psychotherapy recently, due to a number of factors, not the least of which is the limited and limiting understanding of the mind on the part of the average therapist. A guru, by comparison, is expected to have a thoroughgoing knowledge of a canvas far larger than that of the typical college graduate. The transformation of the patient or disciple is commensurate with the wisdom of the therapist or guru, and here in the Gita we are working with a teacher of unparalleled stature. He has demonstrated in the preceeding ten chapters that he is a knower of every aspect of existence. We could only hope that all guides brought similar credentials to their meeting of the minds!

There are few guides who can gently lead another person to the verge of a breakthrough and then know exactly how much to either push or step aside at the moment of truth. I have seen and heard of many cases where a mediocre therapist takes a patient halfway through recovery and then stops or, more commonly, continues to rehash the same painful territory as long as the payments continue. A patient may also lose heart at a stressful moment and abandon the investigation. One has to go all the way "there and back again" to be properly cured, and we all suffer to some degree from the malaise of not digging deep enough.

Another factor for the decline of talk therapy is that words are essentially signs representing ideas, not the ideas themselves. It is not unusual for people to mistake the map for the territory and never actually go anywhere, since reading the map captivates their interest. But it would be a shame to also mistake a crudely drawn map for an accurate representation of what it depicts, as often happens.

A single idea can have multiple words representing it in all the languages in the world, leading to cross-cultural and even intratribal confusion. But "a rose by any other name would smell as sweet," as Shakespeare says, meaning the reality of something is the same despite its varied descriptions. On the other hand, when a person's confusion is destroyed by the use of words, as Arjuna claims here, the unconfused remainder is the field of the Absolute. Taking the small step and giant leap from the idea of the Absolute to the experience of it is a like a rocket trip to the moon after dreaming about it for generations. Words and their concepts that come closest to the essence of what they stand for offer this potential. Still, some sort of leap into the unity of idea and essence remains to be accomplished.

Raw experience is something we have almost forgotten in our love affair with verbiage. As infants we experienced everything directly and intensely, but as we learned to mediate our experience with thoughts and their attendant words we became "sophisticated." Early in life we excelled at interpreting our lives in simple terms that we and others could easily comprehend and appreciate, but then we lost the knack as we were forced to substitute abstractions for direct experience. This parallels Arjuna's entrapment in the snares of social convention that he listed in the very first chapter, and which impelled him to turn to Krishna for advice—strict religious beliefs, morality, racism, violence and war mongering, materialism, burdensome family ties—problems that still vex us today and are if anything more grievous than ever.

As we grow older, vivid experiences become more and more rare. Memories flood in automatically to compare what is presented to awareness with past experience. Fully mediated experience is dull, lacking zest. When all we can do is interpret the new in terms of the old, we slide into senility. Before long death comes to liberate us from our folly, quite possibly to give us a fresh start and a new lease on life. Who knows? But such a fate is not for Arjuna just yet. He has opted for stepping out of the rat maze of expected outcomes and into the rushing stream of the immediate present.

THE ORIGIN AND DISSOLUTION OF BEINGS HAVE ALSO BEEN HEARD BY ME IN ELABORATION FROM YOU, O KRISHNA, AS ALSO YOUR UNEXPENDED GREATNESS.

Arjuna lays it on a little thicker, acknowledging his teacher's value preparatory to requesting the supreme vision. At the beginning of his discipleship he merely asked Krishna to advise him on how to act in a baffling situation. Gradually he has progressed to the point that he is now going to beg to see behind the curtain into the inner workings of the universe. Previously he was dependent on so many things—on his social role, his needs and desires, his intellectual awareness—but now he is prepared to become fully independent and leave them all behind, if only for a short while, so he can learn what freedom feels like.

It is one of the many paradoxes of this earthly realm that the agents of bondage—words—can also be tools of liberation. Yet on closer scrutiny this is logical. To escape a trap we must go out the way we came in. As in the ancient folktale, we can use a thorn to remove a thorn stuck in our foot. But once the injurious sliver is removed the healing happens on its own. Or as chapter VI puts it, "yoga takes its course painlessly."

Arjuna's declared liberation from confusion is a sign that under his guru's guidance he has freed himself from the oppression of a number of psychological thorns. His impending experience will launch him into a new type of exalted confusion that he hasn't even dreamed of, but for now he has been cured of his original malaise.

As we will see, the words of this chapter are doing their utmost to indicate that which transcends their limitations. They may also imply that the magical brew of soma is being imbibed by Arjuna to assist in the changeover, though it is not specifically mentioned. As noted earlier, we have only a suspicious similarity to a "typical" psychedelic trip, if there is such a thing, and the historical fact of soma ingestion as an integral part of ritual practices in those far off, far out times.

After undergoing the experiences put forth in this chapter, in which he outstrips the descriptive possibilities of the mind for a time, and thereby breaks the bonds of his upbringing and acculturation, Arjuna will spend the rest of the Gita reintegrating his vision, learning how to comprehend his experience in new words and concepts so that he can function optimally as part of his society and his world. Some visionaries remain floating in the emptiness of interstitial reality that we call space; others return to share their wisdom with their fellows back on Earth. It's a matter of taste and predilection, but a finalized teaching must include directions for the return trip just in case. It's a poor space program that would send you to the moon with only a one-way ticket!

VERSE 3

SO IT IS AS YOU HAVE SAID
YOURSELF, SUPREME LORD;
I DESIRE TO SEE YOUR DIVINE FORM,
O SUPREME PERSON.

How many people simply accept what they hear in church or read in a book, nod their heads, and go on about their business? They are "believers," and their approach is "please don't upset our beliefs with anything vivid." Arjuna is different. He has heard all about it; now he is dying to see for himself. He wants to make the teachings his own, as realized experience. Until he does this he remains a mere parrot or sheep, or at the very least a neophyte.

Other than its underlying falseness, the main problem with unquestioning obedience or rote repetition is that it makes a person vulnerable to the manipulations of others. Psychologist Alice Miller has made an excellent case that the Nazis' success in Germany was due in large measure to strict obedience training for the young. Children were raised to deny their own truth and kneel before authority, first parental and then social, so when that authority turned vicious, whatever reservations they might have had were overridden by their learned impulse to comply. Their acquiescence meant they were only doing what they had been groomed to do. They were "well behaved" by the standards they had been taught, even though their behavior itself was insane and incredibly cruel.

Human history is filled with similar disasters brought on by willing followers who should have known better. Clearly we must break out of the sarcophagus of bound behavior and reclaim our aliveness. We must rediscover authentic experience and dare to make our own decisions and draw our own conclusions. The Gita is always headed in this direction, as shown by Krishna's final advice to Arjuna: "critically scrutinizing all, omitting nothing, do as you like."

Because of this, it is a methodological necessity that Arjuna request the vision and also that he be granted it.

IF YOU THINK THAT IT IS POSSIBLE FOR ME TO SEE IT, THEN DO YOU, O MASTER OF YOGA, SHOW ME YOUR NEVER-DECREASING SELF.

However it comes about, realization must be accompanied by the surrender of our static mind-set. As long as we cling to what we believe we know, we cannot get outside ourself. Here Arjuna surrenders himself fully into the care of his beloved guru, someone he has learned to trust over a long and respectfully skeptical apprenticeship. Usually surrender is a tentative gesture. For it to succeed it must be completely unrestrained. Wholehearted.

As already noted, the parallels between what Arjuna is about to experience and a psychedelic drug trip are uncanny, and it would be irresponsible of me to disregard them. At the same time we cannot ignore the negativity with which psychedelic trips are often viewed. What was once sacred is often treated as sacrilege now. As always with what I write, readers are free to decide for themselves.

One of many reasons for the suppression of what has been learned in the past from psychedelic drug use, along with banning the medicines themselves, is that a lot of the experimentation in the modern era was unguided and thus chaotic or even occasionally harmful. Later it was learned that most of the reported harm was fictitious propaganda or had been caused by other, more dangerous drugs. In fact, the modern-day relatives of the ancient soma of India are surprisingly benign, and even more so when "used as directed" and under the care of an experienced helper.

The importance of a guru, nowadays more often called a guide, cannot be overestimated. The unknown territory of the mind is vast and full of pitfalls, dead ends, and other dangers. How many of us would strike out into the Amazon rain forest on our own, with little or no preparation? But many carefree young adults have done just that with respect to the jungle of their unconscious. It is a testament to the benignity of psychedelics that so few problems actually occurred. Yet who would risk potential trouble if help were readily available?

Arjuna is wisely asking for guidance from his guru, and not just to prevent disasters. It is easy to miss much of value while traveling in subtle realms. A guide can help reveal significant ideas, but most importantly they can redirect confused thinking into more profitable regions. As Arjuna has come to fully trust his guide, he can defer to him with confidence. Equally important, though not always acknowledged, is that the guru has to trust the disciple just as much. In the course of their long association, Krishna has come to know Arjuna inside and out and has no doubt that he is ready enough for the upcoming experience. His familiarity will be crucial in taking appropriate corrective measures if Arjuna freaks out and gets weird.

Arjuna addresses Krishna as a Master of Yoga not because his body is especially flexible but because he is permanently grounded in the state of oneness. Yoga means always connecting the apparent chaos of the world with the cosmic unity at its core, and Krishna is about to impart a cataclysmic vision of unity that Arjuna will never forget. As a Master of Yoga, Krishna will be the stabilizing anchor for Arjuna's canoe in the upcoming flood. Popular forms of yoga as practiced today are another matter entirely.

Anyone taking a trip is highly vulnerable to suggestions, and it would be shameful but very possible for someone to press their own convictions onto the journeyer. It happens in religious and political institutions all the time, where it's known as brainwashing. Coming to know and trust your guide is similar to attaining bipolarity with your guru. It takes time and thoughtful preparation. Arjuna's respectful dedication demonstrates the proper, wide-awake frame of mind with which to begin.

Finally, any intense experience must be entered into with clear intentions. How often have those who had revelations on LSD thought, "Wow! If I could just turn everybody on to this it would solve all the world's problems!" Unlike an interpersonal spiritual transmission, with drugs you can just slip somebody a pill and away they go. Occasionally this urge has been acted upon. But the soaring sense of kindness and love experienced on an intentional trip is not likely to happen by accident. Entering the unbounded state unprepared can bring a thousand forms of terror. Part of a correct mind-set is knowing what has caused the unsettling state of awareness and that it will wear off eventually.

I well recall some trips where entire dimensions were revealed at the speed of light, over and over, seemingly endlessly. It knocks the ground right out from under your feet, believe me. Knowing that I would "come down" in a few eons was reassurance against the mind-melting fear that being lost in infinity can breed. It seemed impossible that I would ever emerge from the maze, yet naturally and of its own accord it happened, as the drug wore off. Having a guide present to remind you of this eases away the fear and replaces it with a sense of security to enable eager exploration. Alone and unprepared, you might lose your way and miss some valuable learning opportunities as well.

A proper basis for a successful trip requires attention to what are called the *set* and the *setting*. *Set* refers to the state of mind with which you begin, which tends to be greatly amplified as the trip progresses. A sour state of mind will most likely lead to a sour outcome, a bitter mind-set to a bitter adventure, sweet to sweet, and so on. *Setting* means the immediate environment, which also has a profound effect on the nature of the experience. The impact of set and setting will be discussed in more depth in verse 23 and elsewhere.

VERSE 5

KRISHNA SAID:
BEHOLD, ARJUNA, MY FORMS,
BY HUNDREDS AND THOUSANDS,
VARIOUS IN KIND, DIVINE, AND OF
VARIED COLORS AND SHAPES.

As his psychological and conceptual preparation is now complete, Krishna instantly grants Arjuna's request to have a direct experience of the Absolute. Like a magician he sweeps his arms apart and cries, "Behold!" It is left to our imagination how the mystery is revealed; merely reading that the guru shows or enlightens the disciple doesn't actually tell us anything.

Catholic theologian Thomas Merton points out that true revelations must come as a gift, lest they be tainted by our own limitations. In *The New Man* he writes: "The meanings we are capable of discovering are never sufficient. The true meaning has to be revealed. It has to be 'given.' And the fact that it is given is, indeed, the greater part of its significance: for life itself is, in the end, only significant in so far as it is given."[3] While the revelation is granted from without, in a sense, opening oneself to it is the task of the seeker.

Vision quests, fasting, extreme exercise, self-infliction of pain, self-abnegation, sensory deprivation for extended periods, and many other techniques have been shown to help bring practitioners to the verge of the radically renormalized mentality described here. Neuroscientists can think of the experience as one where the "right brain" temporarily becomes dominant, which most often occurs when stress suppresses parts of the left hemisphere, as in a stroke. Many spiritual techniques may simply help practitioners to bypass left hemisphere dominance so they can reexperience the oneness of the so-called right brain. Ideally the goal is a globally awakened brain with the left and right hemispheres harmoniously in balance.

Another angle just being explored in brain studies is that our inner "guidance system" resides in the deepest parts of the brain. The topmost region of the cortex is responsible for our most sophisticated abilities and is what we identify as our consciousness, but it is incomplete. It floats on top of the emotional and survival mechanisms that appear to have evolved earlier. It may be that spiritual techniques quiet the cortex and allow us to bring the light of consciousness into these deeper parts of our makeup, which may well harbor our genius propensities, spiritual sensibilities, and more. Rationalists often scorn these deep levels, because they are asocial and include violent aspects, but I would like to propose that they are much more than that. This is where the intelligence that regulates our metabolism, and possibly the coherent unfoldment of our life, resides. Losing conscious contact with it has put us at the mercy of external forces that often do not have our best interests in mind. Finding a way to reacquaint ourselves with our inner intelligence and integrate it with our conscious mind is an important aspect of spiritual development.

The Bhagavad Gita is a comprehensive textbook on yoga. In it, yoga is presented dialectically, as the joining together of opposites—the thesis and antithesis—into a unity that is greater than the sum of its parts, known as the synthesis, which in the Gita context is realization or enlightenment. The neutrality attained by viewing both sides of a proposition symmetrically reveals the Absolute at its core. The Absolute is thus the synthesis of every dialectic, as well as the realization of yoga. Numerous examples of dialectical polarity appear throughout the Gita, as one of its open secrets.

For that reason, the Gita's dialectical approach to truth is philosophical, rather than strictly scientific or religious. All of these approaches are a search for a true understanding, but philosophy—the love of wisdom—is the synthesis that integrates the knowledge of both science and religion, or physics and metaphysics. Philosophy's highest realization comes from the integration of the two more polarized disciplines, and philosophers are free to embrace truth wherever they find it, whereas proponents of science and religion, locked in their carefully guarded parameters, frequently butt heads. While it often makes references to both psychological and religious imagery, the Gita simultaneously transcends their limitations.

There is a clear implication in Arjuna's upcoming soma trip that the dialectical polarity of conscious and unconscious is resolved when the unknown is brought into awareness. While much is revealed at each incursion, the territory is so vast that consciousness can only investigate a little at a time, although every step may feel like "total realization."

Whatever union with the Absolute may be taken to mean, the Gita emphasizes that it can be brought about gently, without stressing the body or pushing it to the verge of death. The Gita's yoga is the easy, nonviolent route. Its premise is that attaining a dynamically neutral state of mind opens the door to a transformative vision. Psychedelic exploration with proper preparation is similar in being gentle and safe and not requiring the sacrifice of good health. When I speak about the particular method of using psychedelics in reference to Arjuna's intense experience, please consider it to be inclusive of any and all efficacious techniques. The path of the Absolute may be followed from every possible angle, as Krishna assures us in several places, most notably verse 11 of chapter IV, which reads, "As each chooses to approach Me, even accordingly do I have regard for him. My very path it is, O Arjuna, that all men do tread from every (possible) approach."

It is important to keep in mind that *neutral* does not mean "empty" or "vacuous." Just as in mathematics, yogic neutrality takes place when the sides of the equation are equalized, or the polarities in a conflict are brought into balance. Nothing is left out. Rather, neutrality energizes us to be fully and intelligently engaged with every aspect of our life.

The scales of justice aptly symbolize yogic neutrality. When both sides of a conflict are given equal weight it demonstrates a fair decision; the more unequal they are, the less justice is served. Balance scales are also used in the marketplace. The weight of the produce is correct when the scales balance and incorrect when they do not, even though each side contains a totally different substance: one vegetable and the other graded lumps of metal, say. Neutrality is dynamic and embraces all aspects of the situation. When we favor one side, usually "our" side, it conveys a subtle injustice to the entire situation that in the long run harms us far more than the demands of equality ever could.

The vision Krishna is beginning to unveil is going to be wild and crazy, and it will become increasingly revelatory as it unfolds. Arjuna is going to have a hard time keeping his balance! Incipient stages of the psychedelic experience are lit with spectacular colors and rapidly modulating imagery, only faintly reflected in the most outlandish art of the human race, mandalas, op art posters, and so on. It is said that meditating on a mandala can bring you to enlightenment, but it's more probable that traditional mandalas are, like their modern counterparts, attempts to reproduce some faint echo of the visions that the artist personally experienced while tripping. As bizarre as most psychedelic paintings are, the flowing imagery of the trip is thousands of times more intense, and it is capable of changing completely in the blink of an eye. Like synesthetes, people who are known to see sounds and hear colors, a person undergoing a psychedelic experience often experiences synesthesia, where the colors and patterns are viscerally palpable and dancing in synch with any inner or outer music that is playing.

Psychedelic visions have been described as hallucinations, especially by the uninitiated, but—while highly imaginative—they are far from unreal. In a way the mysteriously encoded picture-language that suffuses the brain all the time, the product of a lifetime of sensory experience, is unleashed in a torrential and highly artistic flood. It is possible to intuit much about our mind from watching the imagery, but the display is so gripping and absorbing that coherent conceptualization is only possible after the experience comes to a close. The word *psychedelic* itself means "mind manifesting," by the way, and I use it intentionally in that sense.

Verse 6

Behold the Adityas, the Vasus, the Rudras, the two Asvins, and also the Maruts; behold many marvels never seen before.

After the initial play of colors, a proper spiritual trip moves quickly into more cosmic realms, although visual effects may persist throughout. In this verse we begin to encounter demigods, who are the personification of natural principles. Decoding what the names stand for reveals that they are, among other things, stages of a psychedelic experience. There is immersion in white light (Adityas); unity with the core structural elements of the world (Vasus); mental distress (Rudras), occasioned by the yawning gulf between the psychedelic state of mind and conventional reality; insight into truth and the meaning of life, especially of one's own destiny (Asvins); and finally, appreciation of the divinity of all beings (symbolized by the Maruts).

All these exotic beings except the Asvins were specifically mentioned in the previous chapter of the Gita, where Krishna taught that he was the essential core of each, and all will take a final bow in verse 22 of this one. Here Krishna is at last revealing to Arjuna what he only briefly described before; now actual suns (Adityas are "cosmically brilliant lights") are rising in the firmament of Arjuna's consciousness, one after the other. Their intense white or clear light causes all separate objects and thoughts to melt together into a state of unity.

Whatever intellectual ideas about oneness Arjuna held before, now oneness is an undeniable fact, a berry in the palm of his hand. The certitude induced by an experience like this is indisputable, palpable, pulverizing of all doubts. Sanjaya, the narrator of the Gita, will describe this most classic of visionary experiences from his more circumspect perspective in verse 12.

A trip doesn't build up to "seeing the light" gradually; there is a short period of the play of colors and then almost immediately the shining oneness bursts through. The trajectory of a good trip is like fireworks, which shoot up as rockets to explode in the sky and then slowly burn out and settle back to Earth.

In this heightened state of awareness there is additional synesthesia where the elements (Vasus) become tangible. In an exalted mind-set the yogi—the practitioner of wisdom yoga—"becomes one" with the water of a stream or the flame of a fire, for instance. Not that the yogi actually turns into water or fire, but the mind is captivated so completely by what it perceives that the sense of being a detached observer is temporarily erased. The reality of what the senses are registering is more alive than ever before. It is not uncommon to even feel at one with nature in its entirety, which is a supremely uplifting sensation.

A lot has been written regarding the link between the burgeoning of global ecological awareness and the psychedelic insight that we are intrinsically connected to a greater whole. Recently, the Multidisciplinary Association for Psychedelic Studies (MAPS) ran an entire issue of their magazine on psychedelics and ecology. In it, President Rick Doblin writes:

With psychedelics and ecology, the connection is so direct and fundamental and so inherently present that it requires no intellectual acrobatics to perceive the connecting threads. Albert Hofmann, the inventor of LSD, spoke about the connection between psychedelics and ecology to psychiatrist Stanislav Grof during an interview in 1984. He said, "Through my LSD experience and my new picture of reality, I became aware of the wonder of creation, the magnificence of nature and of the animal and plant kingdom. I became very sensitive to what will happen to all this and all of us." According to Craig Smith, the reporter who wrote Albert's New York Times obituary, "Dr. Hofmann became an impassioned advocate for the environment and argued that LSD, besides being a valuable tool for psychiatry, could be used to awaken a deeper awareness of mankind's place in nature and help curb society's ultimately self-destructive degradation of the natural world."

Doblin continues:

The link between psychedelics and ecology comes primarily from the long-term changes in attitudes and behaviors flowing from these mystical experiences, which of course can and do occur sometimes in therapeutic studies and can certainly be produced without the use of psychedelics. These are core human experiences that psychedelics can help facilitate. The essence of the mystical experience is a sense of unity woven within the multiplicity, forging a deeply-felt and unforgettable common bond between humans, other life forms, nature and matter. This common bond can generate respect and appreciation for the environment, for caretaking and wonder.[4]

All this and more is implied in the concept of the Vasus.

The Rudras or "tragic storms" can likewise appear during a trip. There is often a period of intense shake-up as the false underpinnings of a person's mental orientation are swept away in a flood of new insights. Many times a psychedelic journeyer will experience their whole body, their conceptions, their relationships to people around them, or even the entire world dissolving into nothingness. It can be a dreadfully terrifying deconstruction, but if done on the platform of a stable mind-set it allows the inner suns to shine more brightly than ever. When much of what was previously imagined about reality turns out to be false, its dissolution is a blessing in disguise. The worst pain comes from trying to hold on to ideas that are being stripped of all sense. The harder we try to cling to them, the more pain we cause ourselves. As the Buddhists advise, just let the intense energy pass through you. If you don't resist you cannot get hurt.

After the Rudra freak out of what may seem like a "bad trip" passes, which may be long after the medicine itself wears off, those who have fully processed the experience realize how valuable it was. Likewise, a chaotic, unpleasant meditation is often far more constructive than a pleasant, untroubled one. However, it is possible to defend your position strongly enough to block the processing of the causes of misery, which can lead to a persistent sense of dread or anxiety. The cure is to gird your loins and wade back in, into the very thing that you most want to avoid. If you don't have the resolve in advance to face these difficult Rudras, or what we now call traumas, it is better to not put your foot in the water at all.

The twin Asvins are offspring of the sun, and they are considered the physicians of the gods. One is Satya, meaning "truth, validity, or actuality." On a good trip the first profundity is a sense of absolute conviction. Doubt evanesces like fog before a brilliant sunrise. Ordinary states of mind can be comparatively trivial or at least partial and dubious, but the enlightened state is indelibly real through and through. It is inexplicably self-ratifying. In it, the very aliveness of reality is so uplifting and beautiful that you cannot help laughing out loud with relief and delight. Being restored to truth is possibly the most rehabilitating balm there is. The truth attained during a profound experience is not based on the recognition of specific things, which may be highly embroidered during a trip, but emerges from an inner certitude grounded at a deeper level than sense perceptions.

The other Asvin is Dasra, whose name means "accomplishing wonderful deeds or giving marvelous aid." Further into a trip saturated in truth, there is often a period of insight about the meaning of one's life, including impediments and unrealized potentials. Many of the life-transforming effects of soma ingestion happen at this stage. Knowing yourself more profoundly than ever, a sense of purpose often replaces a former hesitancy.

It is little wonder that these two demigods are considered "physicians," since they heal many deep-seated wounds of the psyche instantly and almost painlessly. Knowing who we are and where we are going has to be the most important insight anyone can have for finding their way through life. Without that self-knowledge we may be drawn from illusion to illusion in a fruitless search, made ever more desperate by a nagging suspicion that we are wasting our gifts.

The Maruts are "the shining ones, the divine sparks." After the instructive phase of the trip, the yogi can see how every separate item of the universe glows with its own inner radiance, its own inimitable value. The new awareness gained is applied to each aspect of the environment in turn, and each becomes exalted, transformed from darkness to light, from stagnation to vivacity. One of many possible examples is the aforementioned heightened appreciation of ecology that has emerged from psychedelic drug use. Ordinarily, humans don't seem to have much trouble taking the earth for granted and grinding it under their heels. Twentieth-century trippers were imbued with a visceral sense of the importance and even sacredness of their environment, and an entire restorative movement was born.

All these marvels are described by Krishna as "never seen before" because they spring from the unique mind of each viewer. There are no Rudras or any of the other demigods anywhere in the "real" world; they stand for aspects of consciousness. While what they represent may occur in a generally similar way in most people, their precise display will be tailored to each person's individual makeup.

The bliss of the Absolute has often been described as ever-new joy. It can never become stale or redundant, because it is never the same. The pleasure of repetitive familiarity via memory is of another order entirely. There are no replays in real life, and even memories are different at every recall. As in surfing, each wave breaks but once, and no matter how similar it is to past waves, it must be ridden wholly in the present or the surfer will wipe out.

NOW BEHOLD HERE IN MY BODY
THE WHOLE WORLD, INCLUDING
THE STATIC AND THE DYNAMIC,
UNITIVELY ESTABLISHED, AND
WHATEVER ELSE YOU DESIRE TO SEE.

Enlightenment is often thought of as a sudden transformative event that changes a seeker into a seer in the twinkling of an eye. The literature is replete with entrancing stories of instantaneous awakening. Vested interests claim that realization is a rare accomplishment that can only be obtained from sources they endorse. Yet to be alive and aware beyond our immediate self-interest is to be enlightened to a degree. Enlightenment is something we all experience at times, but since we've become overly focused on our inadequacies we rarely recognize it. When we once again tune in to our native enlightenment it can strike us as an unbelievably exciting event, but that's primarily due to relief over the sweeping away of our illusions. The light was always there for us to see by. As the Gita says, this is easy. It's so easy, you're already there. You just don't realize it yet.

Anyone who takes a psychedelic medicine will of course undergo a very rapid change in their mental state, but this is primarily due to the removal of inhibitions guarding something that is already present. Because the change comes from a drug effect, it is more or less temporary. The medicine grants a preview of our higher Self, but as it wears off the curtain comes down once again. Becoming firmly established in what we have glimpsed is the aim of a yogic reorientation of mind, which is usually a much more gradual process.

The reference in this verse to "the static and the dynamic" (*sacaracaram*) is a good example of the paired compound extolled in chapter X, verse 33, as an attribute of the Absolute. It is formed of a word and its exact antonym, joined into a single concept that is more profound than if both are considered separately. Ordinarily we distinguish between animate and inanimate objects, but with the eye of enlightened vision, such distinctions instantly vanish. Below the surface, all things are seen to be almost unbearably alive. This is true scientifically also, as everything consists of the same cloud of atomic and subatomic particles, and every atom is a dynamo filled with inexhaustible energy. To the yogi or a person tripping on LSD, the absurd notion that anything could be inanimate produces gales of laughter. They are witnessing everything in intense living activity.

Oddly, most commentators omit or downplay the word in this verse meaning "unitively established," *ekastham*. An exception is Sri Aurobindo, who correctly grasps that this is the most important point of all. He says, "This then is the keynote, the central significance. It is the vision of the One in the Many, the Many in the One—and all are the One. It is this vision that to the eye of the divine Yoga liberates, justifies, explains all that is and was and shall be."[5] Oneness has to be understood as the hub upon which all else turns. Yoga, soma, or whatever the path taken, eventually brings the seeker to a profound realization, and the essence of that realization is the unity of all things. As already noted, this is not an intellectual appreciation but a fully living, direct grokking of the truth of unity, which is an overwhelming experience to anyone who has spent years oppressed by the idea that they are separate and unconnected to the world. The sense of oneness comes in a rush, accompanied by a surge of loving feelings, bringing an overpowering sense of relief from anxiety, soaring optimism, and many other delights. The bliss of conversion of intellectual ideas into living truths is endlessly uplifting.

An important detail is that Krishna tells Arjuna he is free to behold whatever he desires to see. In fact, we always see things colored by who we are, how we think, and what we desire or are interested in. The Absolute alone is formless and pure—contentless in a way. Like a mirror, we see only ourselves in it when we are fortunate enough to have a look. Because of this, Arjuna's reaction to his experience will display overtones of the battle-field, where he is still standing and receiving instruction from his embodied guru. We must not forget that this is Arjuna's coloration of the Uncolored and not some particular attribute of the Absolute itself. The greatest folly that humans are prone to is to project our own limitations or inclinations on God or Nature, thereby magnifying them out of all proportion. That's one reason humility is such an important part of the training: it teaches us to subtract our projections from our experience as a matter of course.

This is actually a critical factor that should be anticipated by anyone embarking on a vision quest of any type. Connecting with the Absolute engenders such bliss that everything seen appears within a nimbus of blessed truth. The truth part comes from our core of the Absolute, but the superimpositions we project upon it are of our own making. Because of their grounding in bliss, our projections can have such a ring of authenticity that we may be unable to shake our convictions in even highly absurd notions that are associated with the experience.

For example, some who take psychedelic medicines permit all their values to be stripped away. Because several false values are seen as utterly ridiculous, values as a whole are intentionally discarded. This can lead to harmful behavior, including the commission of serious crimes. Selfishness and criminality is latent in the unconscious of everyone, and it is very important to retain our value assessments to prevent injury to others or even ourselves. We have to learn how to let go of false values while retaining the beneficial ones. Simply put, we must not throw the baby out with the bath water!

The remaining chapters of the Gita are a textbook on how to sift out the truth from our projected and often cherished falsehoods. It is a very difficult and complex process, and outside assistance is crucial. While the Gita is an excellent aid, spending time with a guru or thera-pist should be considered mandatory, lest the ego corrupt the healing process into narcissism or a messianic complex.

VERSE 8

BUT IF YOU ARE UNABLE TO SEE ME WITH THIS YOUR (HUMAN) EYE, I GIVE YOU A DIVINE EYE; BEHOLD MY SOVEREIGN YOGA.

While manifestation is the outward form of the Absolute, it usually mesmerizes the observer so much that the underlying reality remains inaccessible. Krishna is about to give Arjuna an extra boost so he can peek behind the curtain. Could this be another sly reference to a divine potion with seemingly magical powers? Or perhaps a special electrifying touch or secret meditation technique? We'll never know for sure. Whatever it is, Krishna is adding something to Arjuna's solo ability that pushes him over the top.

In our imagination we can picture a gathering of seekers deep in an Indian jungle, disciples of a wise elder who has spent the day brewing the soma beverage. As night falls they gather around a fire. Having fasted all day, they eagerly await the ritual passing of the cup that their guru humorously calls "a divine eye." Or perhaps it is just the two, Krishna and Arjuna. At least on a first trip, with many unknowns, it is better to be sequestered far from outside interference. The guru may have to figuratively ride the disciple like a wild bull for many hours, or it may be a wholly silent and peaceful journey. Only time will tell.

In yogic terms, there is a dialectical approach of guru and disciple during the long course of instruction that culminates in the merger of their psyches. The two become as one. In that union, wisdom is transferred to the next generation.

Many disciples have had the experience of their guru reading their mind as if it were an open book. I know that for years I was afraid of my guru for this very reason. He had provided a couple of discreet examples in case I needed them, but it was something you could actually feel. Like many others, I felt completely exposed, naked, in his presence. All the guilt-ridden parts of me that I wanted to hide from view, even my own, would surge into my awareness. It was embarrassing and confusing. So, while ardently desiring the total openness of yoga, my ordinary "eye" was also trying very hard not to see. While this became less and less of a blockage over the years, we never quite achieved a completely unguarded state between us. With my earlier LSD trips, though, there had been nothing but openness. There was no place to hide, no inside versus outside. All such duality was perceived to be patently fictional. So despite my defensive fears I knew I could trust my guru's wise advice even when it didn't seem to accord with my own youthful folly. Thanks to those psychedelic visions I was able to grant him the benefit of the doubt, which opened the door for extensive transformations.

SANJAYA SAID:
HAVING THUS SPOKEN, THEN, O
KING, THE GREAT MASTER OF YOGA
SHOWED ARJUNA THE SUPREME
GODLY FORM.

The narrator Sanjaya comes back into the tale three times in this chapter, in an attempt to provide a neutral witness to the extraordinary events taking place. It's very handy to have a more or less dispassionate description from the narrator in the midst of the Event of all events. Yet we can see that Sanjaya is not perfectly unbiased: he still falls back on describing the Absolute in quasi-religious terms. These are probably as neutral and general as it was possible for him to be in his day, but the rishis were striving to develop a new scientific language, and there was still room for improvement. Yet if you stop and think about it, this is a commendable effort at describing the Indescribable. The author of the Gita is fully aware of the inherent limitations of any art, which can only present a specific form of the Formless. So we shouldn't spend our whole life trying to do away completely with how we look at things. Just enjoy it, as long as it's reasonable.

It's worth noting that verses 10, 13, 16, and 24 contain six words beginning with *aneka,* meaning "many, manifold." They are indicative of Arjuna's opening-up process, his expanding consciousness. Also *drashtum* is repeated throughout the chapter, referring to "what is seen."

We're talking about a direct experience here, real seeing as opposed to imagining.

We can only guess at what Sanjaya is describing. The popular imagination has it that Krishna just waves his hand and voilà, the vision begins. Other stories in other traditions describe a hit on the head or a laser beam from the eyes. As Krishna has already described the Absolute in detail in the first ten chapters, it must be much more than just another discourse. He is *showing* rather than *telling*.

Because of the nature of the vision, it seems highly likely there is some psychedelic medicine being served. But no matter how the state is attained, there are universal aspects in how the brain is affected by and interprets an experience like this. However the initiation is viewed, it reveals a great deal about everyone's psychological makeup.

Later, after the vision comes to an end, both Krishna and Arjuna will assert that it was something never before seen by anyone else. What this implies is that it was Arjuna's own personal vision and not some real, eternal entity being accessed. Many seers have had profound visions throughout human history, but they are all unique to the beholder. Like the universe itself, while the underlying structure is fairly uniform, how it is expressed blossoms forth in infinite variety.

VERSE 10

WITH MANY FACES AND EYES, WITH MANY MARVELOUS ASPECTS, WITH MANY DIVINE ORNAMENTS, WITH MANY DIVINE WEAPONS HELD ALOFT,

Words have ever failed those who attempt to describe the Indescribable, even if they are merely detached observers, if it is even possible to be detached at such a critical moment. To an extent we have to read between the lines of what appears to be a picture of a very odd-looking divine being in this and the next verse, which form a single sentence. The deity in question bears a striking resemblance to Indian representations of the god Vishnu, the sustainer of the universe. Krishna is sometimes thought of as one of Vishnu's ten incarnations, which are spread throughout human history.

Everyone who has ever looked into the void has seen their own soul reflected. In other words, the way their brain has been conditioned by its neural structuring, which is a product of earlier input and development, colors and shapes whatever is apprehended. While a modern Westerner is unlikely to hallucinate a Hindu deity, an ancient Indian is equally unlikely to encounter Mickey Mouse. This means that we should interpret the vision here as being appropriate to Arjuna's mindset and not anything we should expect for ourselves. As each of us is vastly unique, so each trip is original. Each sees from their own perspective. Yet the core radiates the unity praised by all who pass the portals.

While not too hard to conceive, it is nearly impossible to perceive the formless unity beneath its variegated forms. Being necessarily limited, any specific expression can only symbolize the whole, it can never be it. The next chapter will address this paradox, and it will admit that for just plain easiness if nothing else, a relationship to a familiar form is acceptable. Still, in this chapter, when an unhinged Arjuna begs to see the unlimited Absolute reduced to his cherished image of Vishnu, Krishna refuses to comply. This means we must never mistake the form for the content, which is a major blunder. Even if we worship a form, we should never forget that it merely represents the Formless and so is not the Only True Version of it.

Having been raised an agnostic, I myself have no favorite deity and am stuck in meditation with pure amorphous light, though I can see that a personal touch would be most welcoming. Friendly even. Long ago I regretted not having a divine being to relate to, but over time I learned to draw my inspiration from beyond that kind of surface focus. Now it strikes me as arbitrary and even silly, but I respect other people's feelings about it, and I hope they will respect mine. Most people have an Absolute they pay homage to, whether a deity or a scientific or political principle. Vishnu turns out to be Arjuna's favorite image, as we shall see. It's good to know who or what image you are beholden to, because it definitely can warp your perspective. That is precisely why Krishna, standing for the Absolute, does not even acknowledge Arjuna's request for him to shrink himself down to the shape of the great god Vishnu.

Faces and eyes represent perspectives, angles of vision. The initial disorientation of a psychedelic trip is often manifested as seeing things from many different points of view, one after another. We are accustomed to our usual way of looking at things, but suddenly we flash on to many new aspects. As soon as we perceive one we are on to the next. This is a mind-blowing or, better, mind-expanding feature of the experience. We may never be able to cling to a single, narrow way of looking at the world again.

Many travelers see hallucinatory faces, and especially eyes, everywhere they look, but we have to assume these are a kind of eerie projection of consciousness. They are like hidden picture puzzles: you look at an ordinary tree trunk and suddenly there is a leering face! Turn to a rock and there's another! Any reaction you have is quickly blown out of proportion. Projections like these may be a source of some of the myths about the world being peopled with multitudes of invisible beings, fairies, ryls, nooks, and so on. Obviously, projective visions have little or no spiritual significance beyond bringing our inner state of mind out in the open so we can become aware of it.

In a heightened level of awareness it is also common to see spirals or concentric circles everywhere. While often dismissed as phosphenes, artifacts of physical eyesight, they have been widely worshipped across the earth as the "eyes" of gods or goddesses. They are like atomic structures or the conversion of energy into matter made visible. When I have seen them, they were accompanied by the conviction that each one was the center of the universe, demonstrating that the universe has centers everywhere, wherever awareness is brought to bear.

Of course, the center is in the percipient rather than in what is being perceived. We only imagine it is "out there" somewhere.

As to the "aspects and ornaments" being revealed to Arjuna, these may be taken either as specific to Vishnu or in a more general sense. It is very common in psychedelic experiences to see gorgeous, jewel-like colors, and symbolic items from the subconscious may be woven through the excursion in the way James Joyce unobtrusively lodged a mundane artifact in each chapter of *Ulysses*. Regardless, every detail of a trip is a reflection of some aspect of consciousness, personal or universal, and so it could be used as a learning tool. Most often, though, the mind is so utterly inundated by the sheer volume of material that it will have great difficulty in focusing on distinct elements. Recording what is remembered soon after the trip comes to an end can provide valuable material for future analysis.

Divine weapons are those devices—mainly rhetorical—by which problems in life are solved. For instance, a thunderbolt represents the intensification of energy to break through an impasse. A knife dissects a situation so it can be studied in detail, and it also separates the useful from the useless parts, in a process known as discrimination. A sword represents the way the intellect can cut through to the core of any issue. And so on. Further exegesis on weapons will be sprinkled through later stages of the vision.

WEARING DIVINE GARLANDS AND VESTURES, ANOINTED WITH DIVINE PERFUMES AND UNGUENTS, A GOD REPRESENTING SHEER MARVEL, WITHOUT END, UNIVERSALLY FACING.

The narrator Sanjaya adds a few more descriptive touches of a typical deity in the form of Krishna/Vishnu. The garland stands for the inter-connectedness of all things and a whole that is greater than the sum of its parts. The image is of the many individual flowers of life-expression being linked by an invisible thread that gives them added significance. Their coherence with each other provides additional layers of utility and beauty. It is a very common experience with psychedelics to see how everything stands in relationship to everything else, almost as if the hidden thread knitting them together has become visible.

Humans have treated their world as being made up of separate, unrelated elements in order to dominate and abuse it without a second thought. The spiritual vision imparted by contemplative disciplines as well as psychedelics makes it very difficult to maintain the illusion. The environmental movement, for example, is grounded in the awareness of humanity's mutual interdependence with the natural world, in the knowledge that things *matter*. If something impacts you, it is impor-tant. Events that occur in isolation have essentially no meaning beyond themselves; in reality there is no such thing as isolation, except in make-believe. That kind of willful ignorance has wrought tremendous damage nearly everywhere on Earth, not to mention in people's psyches.

Another type of garland, psychological rather than objective, is described by Rene Daumal in a letter to his wife, reprinted in the postscript to his miniature gem, *Mount Analogue:*

> I am dead because I lack desire;
> I lack desire because I think I possess;
> I think I possess because I do not try to give;
> In trying to give, you see that you have nothing;
> Seeing you have nothing, you try to give of yourself;
> Trying to give of yourself, you see that you *are* nothing;
> Seeing you are nothing, you desire to become;
> In desiring to become, you begin to live.[6]

The mind-set of a yogi contains a predisposition to look for connectedness everywhere, particularly where it is not obvious, and by so doing they learn to be more fully alive.

Vestures or clothes symbolize the forms draped about the Formless. The "sheer marvel" of it is well known to all who experience some sort of divine connectedness, where every detail is more amazing than the last. The visual extravagance can be mesmerizing.

Suffusing all the visual and sensual activity, if you can resist being distracted by it, is an atmosphere of supernal feeling, of peace and love and light. It has been described as "Divinity everywhere, with no god anywhere." Whether the experience is a mere intimation of realization or a genuine connection with the underlying reality must be left to the judgment of the person having the experience. At its best it bears the ring of authenticity, ratifying itself and eradicating all doubts about its validity. Such a genuine experience beyond the boundaries of previously explored terrain is impossible to adequately express in words, even as its outward symptoms can be unsettling to casual onlookers. Beneath the verbal incoherence is a transcendent and highly educational coherence. Bystanders or guides should remain open to it, following Jesus's excellent advice to "judge not, that ye be not judged" (Matt. 7:1).

The mystical term "universally facing" reminds us that this vision cannot be comprehended from any specialized or limited perspective; it must be taken as a whole or it can't be what it is.

Perhaps coincidentally, reports of psychedelic experiences frequently mention the instantaneous dissolution of dualistic concepts like outside and inside. Space explorers know there is no such thing as up or down in outer space. Dualistic concepts are all relative, not absolute.

IF THE SPLENDOR OF A THOUSAND SUNS WERE TO RISE TOGETHER IN THE SKY, THAT MIGHT RESEMBLE THE SPLENDOR OF THAT GREAT SOUL.

One of the Gita's most famous verses provides the perfect analogy for the dawning of spiritual illumination. An unbearably brilliant white light that permeates everything is a commonly reported experience in realization. If one sun is too bright to look upon, think of what a thousand suns would be like. For starters it would light up every dark recess of the inside of your head.

Vyasa and other rishis used the word *thousand* in the same way we use *zillion,* to mean "innumerable." Let's face it, a thousand of anything might as well be an infinite amount. You are way past the point of wanting to count them as individual items.

It seems that we are made of light, which is the same as consciousness, which is what we feel as love. When we rediscover our true Self, whose nature is that loving light, it brings an upsurging emotion that feels like a return to our true home. Since we tend to feel like we could never find our way back to where we belong on our own, the return is often accompanied by a boundless sense of gratitude toward whatever enables it, which we will presently see drenching Arjuna in respect to Krishna.

All distinctions of color and form disappear in the presence of intense white light. This is true in all our senses, not just the visual. We temporarily are excused from making any differentiations when the thousand suns rise within our inner landscape.

Ordinary consciousness requires an admixture of light and darkness to function. In both utter darkness and pure light, nothing is visible. Only when darkness and light are blended together in the proper measure is the visible spectrum perceptible. But as darkness is simply the absence of light, light is the source of the whole game. It is spectacularly restorative to our being to reconnect with its source for a period of time, especially if our heart has forgotten what it is. This parallels the image of Vishnu as the light of truth and justice reincarnating whenever darkness threatens to gain the upper hand. Chapter IV, verses 7 and 8, of the Gita read, "Whenever there comes to be laxity in regard to right life, O Arjuna, and wrong coming to assert itself, then I bring about the creation of myself. To protect those who are good and to destroy evildoers, for establishing righteousness, I assume being, age by age." This is the perennial philosophy: that our true nature can never be eradicated; it can only be obscured. There will always be the possibility of our being restored to it.

Vedantins especially are very fond of the analogy between the rising sun and the dawning of realization. Narayana Guru, one of the preeminent modern seers of India and the progenitor of my lineage, offers his own version in verse 35 of his *One Hundred Verses of Self-Instruction* (*Atmopadesa Satakam*):

> *Like ten thousand suns coming all at once,*
> *the modulation of discrimination arises;*
> *the veil of transience covering knowledge is maya;*
> *tearing this away, the primal sun alone shines.*[7]

Note that the guru uses *discrimination* in its traditional sense, as differentiating between the transient and the eternal. This is not the same as my use in verse 10, which refers to discrimination within the transient.

THERE ARJUNA THEN BEHELD THE WHOLE WORLD, DIVIDED INTO MANY KINDS, UNITIVELY ESTABLISHED IN THE BODY OF THE GOD OF GODS.

The notion of the Absolute is monotheism at its best, or better yet monism, having nothing left over or omitted. While Hinduism may look pantheistic from a distance, all the gods represent aspects and powers of creation within the total oneness of the Absolute, *brahman,* as presented in the nonreligious philosophy of the Gita and the Upanishads. This is clearly enunciated in this verse, and it will be further clarified in chapter XV. All the gods, elements, individuals—all of everything—are nothing more than moving aspects comprising the body of the one unmoving substratum.

Anyone claiming to be monotheistic but who grants a big chunk of the business of running the universe to Satan or Iblis, or else sequesters God away from the world, giving it a separate status, is in actuality dualistic or polytheistic. Monotheism means that everything can be traced back to one Source. Its primary implication is that since we are all the same in essence, hostility is counterproductive. When you hate the "other" you are hating yourself and denigrating the creative principle as well.

Science at its best is monotheistic, striving to reduce the universe to a single principle or unitive original event. Its variance with religion is mainly in the name of the unity scientists prefer to use, Nature instead of God, and the amount of intentionality accorded to its absolute principle. In addition, a scientist is supposed to be fearless enough to peek under God's skirts to see what It looks like. Religions tend to counsel unquestioning belief and acceptance, rather than exploration and incisive thought. It should be clear by now that the Gita is much more in the camp of the scientist than the religious believer.

Anthropologist Gregory Bateson, pondering upgrading religion to a more scientific perspective, offers some salient advice along these lines in his book *Angels Fear:*

> Two things, however, are clear about any religion that might derive from cybernetics and systems theory, ecology and natural history. First, that in the asking of questions, there will be no limit to our hubris; and second, that there shall always be humility in our acceptance of answers. In these two characteristics we shall be in sharp contrast with most of the religions of the world. They show little humility in their espousal of answers but great fear about the questions they will ask.
>
> If we can show that a recognition of a certain unity in the total fabric is a recurrent characteristic, it is possible that some of the most disparate epistemologies that human culture has generated may give clues as to how we should proceed.[8]

This is perfectly in keeping with the philosophy of yoga and the guru-disciple tradition, which encourages penetrating questioning and counsels humility in respect of conclusions, which are to be regarded as steps in an unfolding process rather than a finalized posture.

Any psychedelic trip or deep meditation must arrive at unity to be complete. Very often there are partial visions, which can seem awesome enough to cause seekers to rest on their laurels. This is actually a great misfortune, because it brings the quest for truth to a (hopefully temporary) close. We don't hear scientists bragging that since they have unified *some aspects* of the universe they can stop where they are. But religious seekers can be much more timidly complacent and may be content with a mere intellectual appreciation of their favorite scripture or the carrying out of some rote activity. What's more, when a seeker quits, satisfied with a partial vision, that single aspect will be magnified out of all proportion, leading to any number of unpleasant consequences, including but not limited to intolerant fundamentalism, psychosis, criminality, or negative withdrawal from life. Having an experienced guide helps prevent a seeker from abandoning the raft in midstream, so to speak, instead holding up a vision of the distant shore that is to be reached.

More often than not it will take several good trips to arrive at the liberated state psychedelic medicines can potentially reveal. Therapists who have used them for their patients realize that a single trip may jar loose psychoses but not fully resolve them. This can produce fear of going any further and result in abandoning the quest prematurely. The patient can be left with a lifetime of lingering anxiety or worse. It is critical to revisit the problem and not try to ignore it, so that resolution can be achieved.

This concept is applicable to any traumatic event. If a child inhales some water while swimming, say, or falls off a horse, they will rapidly develop an aversion to the activity unless they are led back to it as soon as possible. The sense of joy in doing the sport correctly banishes the fear that the accident generated. Without that kind of direct "therapy" the mind is likely to weave a protective phobia around the cause of the trauma.

It is very possible that the historical Arjuna—if there was one—underwent a substantial series of trips, but for economy Vyasa has compressed his experience into a single description. In any case Arjuna arrives at a complete infusion of unity here, which may have taken him awhile to accomplish, even with his excellent preparation. The reverence and gratitude he will express hereafter spontaneously burst forth in response to this marvelous accomplishment.

VERSE 14

THEN ARJUNA, STRUCK WITH AMAZEMENT, WITH HIS HAIR STANDING ON END, REVERENTLY BOWING HIS HEAD TO THE GOD, AND WITH JOINED PALMS, SPOKE.

Once we shed our outmoded snakeskin of conditioning, the intensity of what we experience can be extremely confusing. All our habitual markers lose their ability to anchor us. We are forced to abandon the presumption of control so thoroughly and abruptly it may feel like we're dying. Happily, we later resurface, "reborn" with a fresh vision of our life's calling, our dharma. In concert with the renewed sense of purpose, a natural inner reverence arises as if it had always been present in our heart. It is such a relief to know why we're alive and that it's not an accident of cold fate. While usually temporary, the gratitude of a brimming heart is the only emotion that can bear the intensity of our reconnection with the Absolute.

In chapter IX, verse 34, at the very zenith of the Gita, Krishna asked Arjuna to bow down to him on all levels—spiritual, intellectual, emotional, and physical—and now Arjuna knows in every cell what that means. "Bow down" does not imply groveling but rather opening up to the additional factor of the Absolute, the whole, of which Arjuna now knows he is a part. The impact of his experience extends from the most sublime heights to the material actuality of being in a body.

Sanjaya's image here is wonderfully evocative of someone in a state of ecstasy. In reality, *samadhi,* union with the Absolute, tends to have little if any physical component. The mind is the sole playing field for the sportive delight of realization.

One amusing side note is Arjuna's horripilation, his hair standing on end. He first manifested this symptom back in I, 29, where it was caused by his stupefying confusion tinged with fear. Here it is an outcome of his ecstasy and relief. Vyasa, the master composer of the Gita, has even counterbalanced this minor detail, using it to symbolize the two poles of Arjuna's conflict.

Following this almost theatrically visual introduction, verses 15 to 50 are all in what is sometimes referred to as the ecstatic or extended meter, where each quarter verse has three additional syllables, lifting the Gita's perfectly regular chant to the heights of a rhapsody. This is nearly two thirds of the total of these special verses in the entire work, indicating we have arrived at the peak of the Gita's song.

VERSE 15

ARJUNA SAID:

I SEE THE GODS, O GOD, IN YOUR
BODY, AND ALL SPECIFIC GROUPS
OF BEINGS, BRAHMA, THE LORD,
ESTABLISHED ON HIS LOTUS SEAT,
AND ALL SEERS AND DIVINE
SERPENTS.

Right off the bat, Arjuna reiterates the most important realization of all: that every category of created things, up to and including Brahma, the god of creation, is subsumed in an all-inclusive unity. Knowing this makes the difference between a life of grim divisiveness posited on survival of the fittest and one of surpassing happiness based on mutual support.

Very often a psychedelic trip begins with a nearly instantaneous realization of the falsity of the apparent separation of parts and the reality of the unitive substratum. People "getting off" on a trip frequently burst out laughing at how obvious it is that we are one. Pretension based on isolationist fantasies is stripped away in a heartbeat. It is as if we knew it all along but were temporarily distracted from remembering by the mesmerizing chaos of everyday life. Now we're back. The Absolute is truly nearer than the near as well as farther than the far, as the Upanishads put it. It is close to our core but far from our cortex.

It goes without saying that any vision of the unitive state is beyond the reach of words. Nonetheless, as verbal beings we are bound to try, and this chapter of the Gita offers a very fine poetic description, highly open-ended. Author Vyasa might have skipped it if he could, but some kind of direct connection with the goal has to be included for the sake of completeness, in any endeavor. So don't spend too much time reading about it—go and have your own adventure. Your vision will be tailored to your understanding, just as Arjuna's is tailored to his. Literally tailored: the vision is fashioned from the whole cloth of each person's own consciousness.

Arjuna's mind-set includes his Vedic religious background along with the more ancient Dravidian context of pre-Aryan India. The former includes the panoply of the gods, while the latter is represented by the *nagas,* the divine serpents, both mentioned here. A unitive vision even ameliorates intractable religious differences, which are seen to be nothing more than different descriptions of the same thing. For truth to be true, it has to be all-inclusive. If my truth differs from your truth, at least one of them and probably both must not be true at all.

The lotus can rest in mud and remain immaculate, so it symbolizes the interface between the manifest and the unmanifest. If the unmanifest is going to "sit" atop the manifest, the lotus is precisely the kind of seat it will need to prevent it from slipping into manifestation itself. Moreover, the "thousand-petaled lotus of light" is the highest or final chakra at the top of the head. (The chakras and their relation to consciousness will be discussed in verse 39.) Arjuna is now seeing "outside" that topmost aperture from his perspective, meaning that his somatic energy has risen all the way up the spine to be released, freeing his consciousness from its bodily ties. The symbol of the god of creation sitting atop a lotus teaches us that our creativity springs from the kind of unbounded vision now pouring into Arjuna. Psychedelics are famous as liberators of creativity, one of LSD's primary uses from the very beginning, in science as well as religion and art.

Kundalini yoga, which consists of directed efforts to unleash this liberating energy, is not specifically mentioned in the Gita, but it is very possibly implied here. The kundalini energy is most often depicted as a snake or dragon coiled up at the base of the spine, and the yoga practice aims to awaken the sleeping beast and have it go zooming up the spinal cord. Psychedelics may have an impact on this also. The tattoos that members of the Ecstasy generation often affix to their lower spines are a conscious or unconscious nod to this center of our individual being.

The imagery of this section rapidly becomes extremely lurid, reflecting Arjuna's excitement as the heavens open up for him. To stimulate your imagination, the Victoria and Albert Museum in London has a rare and fabulous painting of what he's "seeing" on display. One of the best-known visual representations is the cover for the 1967 album *Axis Bold As Love,* by the Jimi Hendrix Experience, featuring Jimi as Vishnu. Maybe you even have a copy stored in a box somewhere. Check it out!

I SEE YOU ON EVERY SIDE,
OF BOUNDLESS FORM, WITH
MULTITUDINOUS ARMS, STOMACHS,
FACES AND EYES; NEITHER YOUR
END NOR YOUR MIDDLE NOR YOUR
BEGINNING DO I SEE, O LORD OF
THE UNIVERSE, O UNIVERSAL FORM!

The essence of time is pure duration: things persist because they are spread out in time. We measure and break up time into segments, but these are only convenient superimpositions on top of the eternal quality of duration. Now Arjuna is experiencing the essential nature of time, free of all arbitrary conditions such as past, present, and future. It is actually a wonderfully liberating feeling, to be unaffected by minutes and seconds, what we call time pressures. This is the "eternity in an hour" of William Blake.

Neuroanatomist Jill Bolte Taylor sketches the outlines of these two aspects of time as understood by modern science in her fascinating book, *My Stroke of Insight:*

> To the right mind, no time exists other than the present moment, and each moment is vibrant with sensation. Life or death occurs in the present moment. The experience of joy happens in the present

moment. Our perception and experience of connection with something that is greater than ourselves occurs in the present moment. To our right mind, the moment of *now* is timeless and abundant. . . .

The present moment is a time when everything and everyone are connected together as *one*. As a result, our right mind perceives each of us as equal members of the human family. It identifies our similarities and recognizes our relationship with this marvelous planet, which sustains our life. It perceives the big pictures, how everything is related, and how we all join together to make up the whole. Our ability to be empathic, to walk in the shoes of another and feel their feelings, is a product of our right frontal cortex.

In contrast, our left hemisphere is completely different in the way it processes information. It takes each of those rich and complex moments created by the right hemisphere and strings them together in timely succession. It then sequentially compares the details making up this moment with the details making up the last moment. By organizing details in a linear and methodical configuration, our left brain manifests the concept of time whereby our moments are divided into the past, present, and future.[9]

It may be that psychedelics inhibit left brain sequencing, thus allowing the right brain, with its focus on the present, to take center stage. I can attest that a short song off the Beatles' *White Album* can last for an eternity, and a single day's trip can take an age. Probably the time sense is retroactively imposed during the recovery period, as it is absent for the peak of a trip.

Whatever the trigger that has set it off, Arjuna's experience is at least eerily similar to a psychedelic trip. While many conditions may stimulate the experience of what we often call the divine—and in the Gita the perfect bipolarity of guru and disciple is unquestionably the highest recommendation—several types of medicine can make the experience available to a broad spectrum of seekers. While there are innumerable descriptions in the psychedelic literature that closely parallel the Gita's poetry, the following from leading mushroom investigator Gordon

Wasson permits us a lot of insight into Arjuna's state of mind. Wasson was very likely the first outsider to participate in the sacred ritual of mushroom ingestion with the Indians of Central America, in the early 1950s:

> The advantage of the mushroom is that it puts many, if not everyone, within reach of this state without having to suffer the mortifications of [some saints]. It permits you to see, more clearly than our perishing mortal eye can see, vistas beyond the horizons of this life, to travel backwards and forwards in time, to enter other planes of existence, even (as the Indians say) to know God. It is hardly surprising that your emotions are profoundly affected, and you feel that an indissoluble bond unites you with the others who have shared with you in the sacred agape. All that you see during this night has a pristine quality: the landscape, the edifices, the carvings, the animals—they look as though they had come straight from the Maker's workshop. This newness of everything—it is as though the world has just dawned—overwhelms you and melts you with its beauty. Not unnaturally, what is happening to you seems to you freighted with significance, beside which the humdrum events of everyday life are trivial. All these things you see with an immediacy of vision that leads you to say to yourself, "Now I am seeing for the first time, seeing direct, without the intervention of mortal eyes."[10]

We can notice Wasson's heavy emphasis on seeing, which echoes Arjuna's highly visual descriptions. Extremely colorful and entrancing scenes are common to both psychedelic experiences and religious scriptures.

Of all the unhappy consequences of social conditioning and its fear of living reality, the proscription against religious experience via mushroom medicines is among the most debilitating for a civilization sorely in need of awakening from its stupefied slumbers.

Verse 17

I BEHOLD YOU WITH DIADEM,
MACE AND DISCUS, GLOWING
EVERYWHERE AS A MASS OF LIGHT,
HARD TO LOOK AT, EVERYWHERE
BLAZING LIKE FIRE AND SUN,
IMMEASURABLE.

Both Sanjaya and Arjuna conceive of the Absolute as Vishnu, in conventional Vedic guise, although Arjuna is about to go far, far beyond his religious conditioning. Later, in verses 45 and 46, he will beg to have his religious sentiments restored. Krishna pointedly ignores his request and instead resumes his form as an "ordinary" friend and guru. This is a clear indication that extravagant religious images are mere window dressing, and at best they are intermediate to a total grounding in the Absolute. Spiritual seekers should take them less, rather than more, seriously.

In the mythological context, Krishna is an aspect of Vishnu, whose diadem and mace are his royal crown and scepter. Vishnu's discus is called *sudarshana,* meaning "beautiful vision." Since a discus is a divine weapon, it means that the inspiration of a high ideal may be directed at obstacles to clear the path to enlightenment. In other words, instead of combating problems and fighting through them, conjunction with the Absolute peacefully guides one's footsteps. Or as noted as early as the second chapter, the vision of the One Beyond dispels the last vestiges of attachment to the ordinary. The power of the discus calls to mind Joan of Arc, so mesmerized by her vision of God that as a teenager she was a major figure in resolving an international political stalemate. Nonviolent resistance is another example, which invokes high ideals to win victories that would likely be impossible through mortal combat.

Most of us have known kind and gentle people who don't seem to even notice obstacles. They pass through them as if they aren't there. Then there are those who are looking for trouble and are bound to find it. Their pugnaciousness and suspicion bring them no end of grief, which they use to reinforce their negative framing of reality. One of the most valuable bits of training a guru can impart is to realign the psyche to see the world as beautiful instead of hostile, because it makes life simultaneously more enjoyable and less problematic.

Many revolutionary enterprises begin with a beautiful vision, but as they meet resistance from the established paradigm they usually begin to make compromises to meet the resistance on its own terms. Before long, what began as a fresh endeavor is converted into a retread of the status quo. Vishnu is the Sustainer, so the beautiful vision he represents cannot be watered down. This means we have to make sure we do not lose contact with the inner truth that inspires our path. There is no better example of this than Gandhi, who stubbornly held to his nonviolent approach even as many around him urged the opposite.

Under the influence of psychedelics, if you are in a stable state of mind, it is very easy to resist provocations. The bliss of immersion is so intense that it annuls any irritation. Unfortunately, as the medicine wears off it leaves you in a more susceptible state for a period, as will be discussed in verse 31. Protracted mental balance will have to be retrieved through diligent effort.

There is a linear sequence to Arjuna's "trip" that can only be observed when the verses are read carefully all together. It begins in a way that he can at least attempt to describe in familiar terms. As it intensifies, it moves rapidly to a vast, all-encompassing experience that erases the ordinary conceptualizations that had previously served him adequately. Shortly he will be flooded with emotionally tinged wonderment. Time will expand to include the end of all the living beings surrounding him on the battlefield. At the peak, he attains to an *agonia,* the agony of divine transformation. Afterward, he is filled with remorse for his former spiritual blindness and resolves from the bottom of his heart to make his newfound realization a living part of his life.

Of course we don't have to relate this to a psychedelic experience, but a "breakthrough" LSD trip quite frequently follows the same general outlines.

YOU ARE THE IMPERISHABLE, THE
SUPREME THAT IS TO BE KNOWN;
YOU ARE THE ULTIMATE BASIS
OF THIS UNIVERSE; YOU ARE THE
UNEXPENDED AND EVERLASTING
CUSTODIAN OF (NATURAL) LAW;
YOU ARE THE IMMEMORIAL
PERSON, I BELIEVE.

Once the psyche breaks through the doors of perception, the light that is the essence of everything pours in. What had been dark is dark no more. It is as though we had been living in a deep dungeon, and now the gates have been thrown open to admit the full light of day. The exuberance of the liberated soul soars like the spirit of a condemned prisoner who has suddenly been granted a reprieve.

This is the "splendor of a thousand suns" rising in the firmament that Sanjaya more dispassionately described earlier. An explosively happy state floods Arjuna's being immediately after the darkness of separation is dispelled. Swept up in it, he knows the light as an unbearably wonderful essence of everything. His heart blazes in response, pouring forth love and gratitude for the simple awareness of existence. The types of thoughts that Arjuna expresses now are typical of a diligent seeker from whom the veil has finally fallen. Krishna has covered all these ideas in detail already, but now Arjuna is feeling the truth of them in the depths of his soul.

We don't realize how the illusion of death hangs over us like a dark cloud until we come face to face with eternity, and then in an instant the pall is lifted. We perceive the illusion only by its absence. Then, knowing that *something* is imperishable, and realizing that we are wholly permeated with that substance, fear is erased. Arjuna will be cosmically terrified later in his trip as he blasts through unfamiliar territory and into what is glibly called the Void, but ever after he will be immunized from the ordinary fears that plague most of humanity most of the time.

The certitude that "This is what is to be known!" is a primary "aha!" moment. A seeker goes through life wondering about many things. Questions and unsolved riddles propel the search. You are searching for the Unknown. And then one day, like diving into a pristine mountain pool, you arrive, finally in direct contact with what has been drawing you all along. The Unknown has become known. Flushed with relief, you think, "Oh, this is what everybody has been talking about!" "This is what religions are carrying on about!" "This is what I've been looking for all my life!" Thoughts like that. And then to know in your bones that this is who you—and everyone else—*are* in essence is a soaring realization. You haven't just been searching for a needle in a haystack, some distant and recondite fact, but for something that is everywhere and every when, immanent and broadly accessible across the whole span of existence. How can it have been so easy to overlook?

In the grip of realization, it becomes clear to you that there is no "guy" somewhere pulling the strings of a puppet universe but that coherent laws permeate the cosmos throughout its entire expanse. How else could it possibly work, vast as it is? But this does not rule out a principle of enlightenment or evolution, which imbues the whole with meaning. The incremental movement from darkness to light, untruth to truth, and death to immortality makes every step significant. It is as Henri Bergson quipped, with tongue slightly in cheek about the machine part, that "The universe is a machine for making gods." And every so often the gradual everyday progress attains a new order of magnitude via a quantum leap like the one Arjuna makes here.

Speaking of quantum leaps, Arjuna's affirmation that these are *his* beliefs tells us that he is no longer just a student. He is in the process of being reborn as a fully sentient adult human, who now has firsthand knowledge to augment the very extensive, but inevitably theoretical, instruction Krishna has been giving him. At last he really *knows* what he knows. He still has plenty to learn from his mentor, but he can now be released on his own recognizance, so to speak. This is the minimum requirement of a "good citizen" that ordinary education promises but usually fails to deliver, and it imparts a bedrock sense of confidence that will sustain Arjuna for the rest of his life.

Probably the most famous scientific study of the mystical impact of psychedelics is the Good Friday Experiment of 1962, where ten Protestant divinity students were administered psilocybin mushroom extract and ten a placebo before attending Good Friday services. All were of the male persuasion. While the initial findings were dramatic enough, a follow-up study was conducted twenty-five years later. Rick Doblin wrote a lengthy analysis that was published in *The Journal of Transpersonal Psychology.* He reported in part that

each of the psilocybin subjects felt that the experience had significantly affected his life in a positive way and expressed appreciation for having participated in the experiment. Most of the effects discussed in the long-term follow-up interviews centered around enhanced appreciation of life and of nature, deepened sense of joy, deepened commitment to the Christian ministry or to whatever other vocations the subjects chose, enhanced appreciation of unusual experiences and emotions, increased tolerance of other religious systems, deepened equanimity in the face of difficult life crises, and greater solidarity and identification with foreign peoples, minorities, women and nature. Subject K.B.'s description of the long-term effects is representative. He remarks:

It left me with a completely unquestioned certainty that there is an environment bigger than the one I'm conscious of. I have my own interpretation of what that is, but it went from a theoretical proposition to an experiential one. In one sense it didn't change anything, I didn't discover something I hadn't dreamed of, but what I had thought on the basis of reading and teaching was there. I knew it. Somehow it was much more real to me. . . . I expect things from meditation and prayer and so forth that I might have been a bit more skeptical about before. . . . I have gotten help with problems, and at times I think direction and guidance in problem solving. Somehow my life has been different knowing that there is something out there. . . . What I saw wasn't anything entirely surprising and yet there was a powerful impact from having seen it.[11]

K.B.'s assessment is close to what we can imagine Arjuna's take to have been, twenty-five years after his vision of the Absolute.

The meaning of a term like *Immemorial Person* in the Gita is, to put it bluntly, "God." The fact that the universe embodies a principle to coax us on to ever more complex states of awareness and ability implies a kind of benevolence that seems almost human, and so, with our anthropomorphic tendencies, godly. There is a mysterious interface between personal and impersonal factors that will be extensively explored in later chapters of the Gita (especially XII and XV). Arjuna's—and indeed most people's—preference is for the universal laws to be personified. While we must guard against the tendency to project our personal desires and fantasies onto the Absolute, it can be very consoling to treat it as a friend and helpmate. In truth, all honest attitudes are legitimate, and the positing of an external factor is one way of avoiding the "I'm hipper than thou" kind of spiritual conceit. After all, our relative merits, no matter how amazing, are quite trivial in comparison with the Absolute. In future chapters the Gita carefully instructs the seeker how to avoid the pitfalls of anthropomorphism in this important matter, while at the same time endorsing its efficacy.

In employing "immemorial," Nataraja Guru renders *sanatanah* a little differently than others, who use "immortal, deathless, undying," and so on. The verse has already featured *aksara,* which means "imperishable," so the latter translations are basically repetitive. With his version, Nataraja Guru brings in the sense of endless time, retroactively as well as prospectively, which is definitely an implication of the Sanskrit word and is in keeping with the thread in the next verse as well.

I SEE YOU WITHOUT BEGINNING, MIDDLE, OR END, OF NEVER ENDING FORCE, OF NUMBERLESS ARMS, HAVING MOON AND SUN FOR EYES, YOUR FACE LIKE A LIT FIRE OF SACRIFICE BURNING THIS UNIVERSE WITH YOUR OWN RADIANCE.

Here the Absolute is recognized as transcending time, and in the next verse, space. Verse 19 should be compared with verse 32, where Krishna categorically states, "I am Time." Absolute time is pure duration, and its beginnings, middles, and ends are a continuous transient play on its surface.

The multiple forces and arms Arjuna speaks of represent the laws of nature, the mind-bogglingly complex extensions of the first principle or "Big Bang" of the universe into every aspect of existence. Whereas in ordinary consciousness we might examine one "arm" at a time, Arjuna views them metaphorically all at once, and the vision overwhelms him. There are far more of them than he ever believed possible. This is the kind of humbling vision that eradicates the common fault of imagining we already know everything. Humans are just beginning to wake up, and we are by no means privy to all the secrets of the universe quite yet.

The first line of the Mundaka Upanishad, II, 1.4 is "Fire is his head; His eyes, the moon and sun." Arjuna is not necessarily waxing rhapsodic and quoting the Upanishads; rather, he is seeing what the rishis of the Upanishads also saw. Moon and sun respectively symbolize consciousness and the radiant spirit that illuminates it and is reflected by it. The third light Arjuna refers to, equating it with Krishna's face, is the sacrificial fire, that which consumes everything, breaking down complex constructs into their component chemicals so that new entities can be formed. It is this last feature that will begin to unnerve Arjuna as his trip continues to unfold. His habitual mental orientation will be dissolved into a more generalized, potential state, so that later on it can be reassembled into more efficacious patterns.

Reading quickly through this chapter makes it seem that all Arjuna's complicated visions are crammed together in close proximity, but we have to assume there is a significant span of time involved, at least for an outside observer if not for him. As anyone who has journeyed on psychedelic medicines knows, time—when it is even perceived—expands exponentially. Arjuna's splendorous vision epitomized in the previous verse would have seemed endless to him, a truly eternal moment. He is still at the peak, but in citing the recycling fire that burns the universe Vyasa has artfully sown a seed of "coming down" here, which will begin to sprout in the next verse.

THE SPACE BETWEEN HEAVEN, EARTH, AND THE INTERMEDIATE REALM IS PERVADED BY YOU ALONE, AS ALSO THE QUARTERS; HAVING SEEN THIS WONDERFUL, TERRIBLE FORM OF YOURS, THE THREE WORLDS ARE IN DISTRESS, O GREAT SELF.

A handy way to conceptualize the universe is that it is the mind turned inside out. Or that the mind is the universe turned outside in. When we think we gaze out upon limitless vistas of time and space, what we're really experiencing are passion plays staged in recondite corners of our own brain. Moreover we have become like overbearing directors who want the play to be performed just the way we have learned to want it and bully the actors so they lose their spontaneity. The illusion of control inhibits the natural upwelling of our dharma, our innate inclinations, and in the process sabotages our vitality.

Scientists observing the brain via fMRI (functional magnetic resonance imaging) can see that thought impulses occur for up to ten seconds before we become aware of them, meaning our consciousness is like a tail firmly convinced it is wagging the dog. A powerful vision like Arjuna is having quells the ego's fantasy of being in charge, at least temporarily, so the inner flow of evolutionary development can rush ahead unchecked. With luck and a stretch of hard work, the visionary territory gained from being a neutral witness of our deeper Self can be annexed permanently. Most commonly, the ego will regain its dominance after the medicine wears off. Hopefully it will be chastened and assume its rightful place as a single late stage of a very complex process. Otherwise, if it tries to resume its top-dog role, the power struggle can be very dangerous, leading to derangement and megalomania. I refer to this as the Al Haig syndrome, after the mid-level cabinet member under U.S. President Ronald Reagan who famously said "I'm in control here" after Reagan was shot, even though he was no better than fourth in the Constitutional line of succession, and no one was looking to him. The ego is a crucial servant but a hazardous master.

Psychedelics and other psychoactive medicines probably suppress some of the left brain inhibitory functions so that we can explore areas of the brain that are normally off limits, like the deep regions where our thoughts actually originate. Unlike alcohol, which stupefies *all* the brain, these medicines apparently have little or no effect on the right brain, with its more unitive orientation. Below both the right and left brain is the brain stem, with its essential life-maintenance role, which is also unaffected.

From the ego's vantage point, the deeper regions of the brain where our thoughts and motivations arise are unknown territory. All that modern cosmonauts need to explore their inner universe is a little dedication and a "ticket to ride." The expensive equipment, teams of experts, tracking stations, and toxic rocket fuel used by physical space travelers to plumb the weary and boring vacuum of outer space are completely unnecessary.

Today we have different names for the "three worlds" that Arjuna describes as heaven, earth, and the intermediate realm. We call these the macrocosm, the microcosm, and the everyday or transactional world. All are endlessly complex and fascinating and filled with potential for amazing discoveries. Note that the Absolute is not equated with space as such here but with the space *in between* those realms. Modern instruments have allowed us to determine that "empty space" is actually surprisingly full, containing whirling atoms and complex organic molecules, photons, dark matter, plasma, and who knows what else. What is meant by "in between" is the true emptiness compared to which even space is a form of manifestation.

There is an inside joke shared by both science and religion. When the scientist looks within a physical object, its molecules consist of mostly emptiness with some atoms scattered through it. Atoms themselves are mostly emptiness with a few tiny particles scattered around, and those particles in turn are mostly emptiness buoyed up by really tiny subatomic particles. These in turn . . . well, you get the idea. Religion looks with the mind's eye instead of the microscope, but the conclusion is the same: this universe consists solely of appearances artfully formed from pure nothingness. The joke is that the nothingness somehow appears to be everything. No one really knows *why* there seems to be something rather than nothing, but everyone agrees that this is the case.

The three realms are not actually in distress, either, any more than usual. The Absolute contains all things, not just their good half. It is Arjuna, just beginning to freak out about what all this means, who is in distress. He is still near the apogee of his trip, but all is not merely sweetness and light anymore. The world that once seemed so constant and fixed is now comprehended to be in continuous tumultuous transformation. One of the mind's primary functions is to provide us with an illusion of stability within the utter chaos of a mindbendingly dynamic universe, where we can never step into the same river twice. We incubate as long as necessary in a calm and sequestered environment, like a chick in its sturdy eggshell. But at some point we have to break out and learn to fly. The transition is not always comfortable or effortless. Part of us longs for the womblike darkness we are accustomed to, even as we stand on the brink of emergence into the light.

VERSE 21

INTO YOU ENTER THOSE HOSTS
OF THE SURAS, SOME IN FEAR OF
YOU MUTTER WITH JOINED PALMS,
BANDS OF GREAT RISHIS AND
PERFECTED ONES HAIL YOU
WITH THE CRY "MAY IT BE WELL!"
AND PRAISE YOU WITH
RESOUNDING HYMNS.

After the initial rush of cosmic relief at discovering what he had been searching for his whole life, afterward tempered with a whiff of sacrificial fire, Arjuna rises to yet another pinnacle. He has broken through his individual isolation to find himself metaphorically in the company of the realized beings of all ages. This is a particularly wonderful stage of a trip. Having tasted the manna of celestial bliss, you know in your heart that it is the same as all enlightened beings have known and been praising, in divergent and creatively artistic fashion, down through the millennia. You have arrived, and you have coincidentally discovered the purpose and meaning of your life. No joy could be greater.

I well remember having my breakthrough on LSD, floating in space supported on pillows of light, which was supremely loving and all-pervasive. The actual world appeared as a filmy veil of insubstantial nothingness barely shimmering atop the glow. As a lifelong atheist, the realization hit me particularly hard that *this* was what the ancient seers were describing in all the spiritual texts. I was in the place they had all struggled to describe. Right then and there—wherever that was—I took a vow to learn how to attain that wondrous state permanently, without the use of drugs, if for no other reason than that they wore off. And the world being the fateful psychodrama it is, before the year was out I "accidentally" found myself at the feet of a true guru, one who was an expert lecturer on the Bhagavad Gita and strongly antidrug to boot. Anything of value in this commentary can be traced directly to his influence and instruction, which in turn were a legacy of his own brilliant guru.

Under conditions of intense emotion, humans often take recourse to prayer, which is a natural way to access their inner strength. Awe can easily turn into fear, when the unknown is immanent. Under stress the ego may become unmoored like a feather in a windstorm, rendering it unable to mount any complex conceptualizations. Ordinary thoughts are impossible, and in any case they are inadequate for regaining stability. For the one of unexamined life, all sorts of deals, contracts, and pleas may find utterance to try to restore calm: "Dear God, please give me what I think I want, and I promise to ____." But for those who have meditated deeply on the meaning of existence, there can only be gratefulness and appreciation for the underlying harmony. Anything less would be carping, or else too trivial to bear. The universe is perfectly perfect, and everything is just as it should be. If you think differently, it's because selfish interests are blocking your vision, not because of any defect in the nature of things. Ups and downs are the natural rhythms of a symmetrical universe, and not the product of divine whimsy or cruelty.

A Christian theologian whose name escapes me agrees that the only legitimate prayer is thankfulness. If you realize what an awesome gift life is, you are compelled to respond with gratitude, even when events are less than comfortable.

The prayer or blessing of the *maharishis,* the great seers, given here is *svasti,* meaning "May it be well!" The name of the auspicious rotating cross or *svastika* is a related word, as "that which gives the blessing (svasti)." For those who are blasted into the Void by the intensity of their realization, a one-word utterance is more than enough. Most often it is even less: the One Syllable *Aum,* or its cognates *Amen* or *Amin.*

By the way, this is the same svastika the Not-Sees—Nazis— perverted into a symbol of racial superiority. Hopefully their degradation of the "cross in motion" is not retroactive. Now that we know with scientific certainty there is only a single human race or species, the Nazi mentality is proved to be doubly bankrupt. The Gita was composed some 2,500 years ago to try to coax the troglodytes of its day into the light, and it is one of the world's greatest masterpieces in favor of universal amity and the abolition of all schisms.

The word *Suras,* referring to the wise or learned sages, is also quite interesting. It is closely akin to Surya, the sun, implying the sages are radiant in their wisdom. The bliss of realization emanates from them like light from a star. Their opposite numbers would be the Asuras, the not-wise, otherwise known as demons. Demonic behavior is a predictable outcome of the absence of wisdom.

THE RUDRAS, ADITYAS, VASUS AND SADHYAS, VISVAS AND THE TWO ASVINS, MARUTS AND USHMAPAS, HOSTS OF GANDHARVAS, YAKSHAS, ASURAS AND SIDDHAS, ALL GAZE AT YOU, WONDERSTRUCK.

Along with the Suras of the previous verse, the whole panoply of divine and semi-divine mythical beings are seen to be enthralled by the Absolute, their common Source. We can think of them as myriad aspects of consciousness. The way some of them fit into the progression of a revelation was presented in verse 6. The rest are mostly of minor importance, except the Gandharvas, the celestial musicians. They are keepers of the soma plant and appear to get high pretty much all the time, either with music or the juice. Or both. They love the sensual life. Music and psychedelics have always made a very happy combination! Among other things, both activate the brain globally rather than locally.

In Arjuna's vision, the whole range of metaphysical beings is stupefied with wonder. This is probably a projection of his own amazement. When we become aware of the Absolute it can immobilize us. No matter how well we might be prepared, the encounter is going to shock us out of our mind for a while. Even after the initial "aesthetic arrest" we are likely to become frozen by conceiving of too many possibilities to sort out. To be able to act coherently again we have to screen out the full awareness of our true nature, and thus we begin to imagine ourselves as separate beings. This may be the defining paradox of existence, that even though we are nothing but the Absolute, we have to forget this fact in order to play the game of life. But once having rediscovered our Self, we begin a return journey as competent adults to gradually recover the awareness of who we truly are.

Over the course of an ordinary life the ego can become like a closed fist, unconsciously clenching its fictitious props in a vain attempt to preserve its illusory self-image. The yogic or psychedelic experience joins the practitioner with a powerful flow that forces the fist to relax its grasp. The changes this unleashes are so intense and rapid fire that the traveler can only surrender to their commanding ministrations. The result is openness to many formerly suppressed aspects of being. It is nearly impossible to plan for being overwhelmed, because by definition the experience must be outside of anticipated parameters. We cannot be overwhelmed and still remain in our comfort zone. A yogi should therefore take a strong resolve to not be held in check by fixed beliefs, as they can easily impede the process of spiritual awakening.

These important spiritual truths have a very practical, down-to-earth side as well. Joe Keohane, writing in the *Boston Globe* newspaper in 2010, reports that recent studies have shown that people resist changing their beliefs even when presented with facts that directly contradict them; in fact, contradictory facts often *reinforce* false beliefs:

Most of us like to believe that our opinions have been formed over time by careful, rational consideration of facts and ideas, and that the decisions based on those opinions, therefore, have the ring of soundness and intelligence. In reality, we often base our opinions on our beliefs, which can have an uneasy relationship with facts. And rather than facts driving beliefs, our beliefs can dictate the facts we choose to accept. They can cause us to twist facts so they fit better with our preconceived notions. Worst of all, they can lead us to uncritically accept bad information just because it reinforces our beliefs. This reinforcement makes us more confident we're right, and even less likely to listen to any new information.[12]

Knowing this, it behooves us to be very careful to minimize our opinions and beliefs and only adopt the most open and well-thought-out ones. It is crucial to be prepared to amend or discard them as new information comes to us. Religious, political, and even scientific dogmatism generally serves as a barrier to intelligent thinking, but we do not have to remain sequestered behind locked doors in our mind. Wonder, however it is achieved, can jolt us out of our stagnation and make us eager to shake off outmoded and unquestioned attitudes.

Jesus is reported to have said, "Except ye be converted, and become as little children, ye shall not enter into the kingdom of heaven." Young children, when properly cared for, live in a permanent state of wonder, and spiritual ecstasy bears a close resemblance to their blissful condition. In many parts of the world, however, adults do their best to convert them out of their natural state with all sorts of draconian disciplines. Exploratory learning is treated as intentional misbehavior and severely curtailed, often in the name of God. This may well be the preeminent reason for the myriad mental ills humans suffer as a species.

Professor of psychology and philosophy Alison Gopnik, writing in *Scientific American,* relates what recent studies have revealed about the importance of the open mind of the child:

> Fundamentally, babies are designed to learn. . . . The lack of prefrontal [cortex] control in young children naturally seems like a huge handicap, but it may actually be tremendously helpful for learning. The prefrontal area inhibits irrelevant thoughts or actions. But being uninhibited may help babies and young children to explore freely. There is a trade-off between the ability to explore creatively and learn flexibly, like a child, and the ability to plan and act effectively, like an adult. The very qualities needed to act efficiently—such as swift automatic processing and a highly pruned brain network—may be

intrinsically antithetical to the qualities that are useful for learning, such as flexibility.

A new picture of childhood and human nature emerges from the research of the past decade. Far from being mere unfinished adults, babies and young children are exquisitely designed by evolution to change and create, to learn and explore. These capacities, so intrinsic to what it means to be human, appear in their purest forms in the earliest years of our lives. Our most valuable human accomplishments are possible because we were once helpless dependent children and not in spite of it. Childhood, and caregiving, is fundamental to our humanity.[13]

Arjuna's soma experience has converted him for its duration into a semblance of a young child: open, filled with wonder, unprejudiced, learning at the speed of light. What a blessing to revisit that state as an adult, where any positive changes can be rapidly made permanent.

For a person who has turned around, however briefly, and become as an uninhibited little child, it is most important to have a wise caregiver on hand to provide guidance until the frontal cortex wakes back up. The lack of inhibition could lead the seeker into danger, and a measure of inhibition eventually needs to be restored, although normal cautiousness can be worn much more lightly than before.

SEEING YOUR GREAT FORM, WITH
MANY FACES AND EYES, OF MANY
ARMS, THIGHS, AND FEET, WITH
MANY STOMACHS, WITH MANY
TERRIBLE TEETH, THE WORLDS ARE
DISTRESSED, AS ALSO MYSELF.

As the vision continues to expand, Arjuna's limited perspective is shattered. As we used to say, his mind is blown. What he sees plainly before him is more than he can comfortably conceive of. While this will expand his horizons in the long run, the sense of customary surroundings being stripped away is hard to deal with. Where we should let go so we can expand to the next level, the urge is to hold on to the known as tightly as possible. At this stage of a trip, many people feel like they are dying. And they are—dying to a small world that can no longer contain them. If they can go with the flow they will find they are being reborn to a greater dimension of who they are.

Set and setting are as important to a spiritual vision as they are to a psychedelic experience. As noted earlier, set refers to the individual's state of mind, including both their deeply fixed cultural and intellectual roots and their mental mood of the day. The setting refers to the "mood" of the environment. Both of these have a profound impact on the type of experience a person has.

Spiritual experience is never "pure" in the sense that it is wholly independent of interpretation on the part of the one having the experience, and any boasting along those lines is delusory. While what is apprehended might be related to the unalloyed Absolute, the whole cannot be either taken in or explained without breaking it into manageable parts, with the essence inevitably diluted by the individual's perspective. The conscious mind is incapable of fully processing the stupendous light that is being revealed, so it will overlay its intrinsic conditioning onto the unconditioned absolute ground. One of the major tasks of spiritual practice is to eliminate as many of the diluting factors as possible, in other words to remove the personal bias from every situation. Our personal *interest* is fine, just not the bias. Other people's needs are also to be taken into account.

Evolution can be considered the universe's ongoing attempt to see itself as it really is, in ever more detail, but as exciting as each leap forward is to the ones doing the leaping, they all have their limitations. The process of refinement of our understanding is apparently infinite. This means we can most accurately envision the Absolute at the core of an experience after we subtract as much as we can of our mind-set and the circumstances attending it.

A great deal of the work Krishna has been doing with Arjuna is designed to rectify his state of mind in this very way, to provide him with the proper set. If Krishna had revealed his Absolute nature to Arjuna when he was still the brash warrior, his experience would have been militaristic in character. If he had shown him the One Beyond while he was miserable and confused at the inception of his discipleship, the vision would have been clouded by his desire to withdraw. The warrior mentality is overly positive and the withdrawal mentality is overly negative. Krishna's subtle psychotherapy has led Arjuna to an optimistic yet neutrally balanced state, which will allow him to obtain the maximum benefit from his present revelation. And throughout the whole trip Krishna is standing by as a compassionate guide to insure that his dear disciple maintains his balance and to protect him from any unwelcome outside influences supplied by the setting.

Despite this careful preparation, it's important to keep in mind that Arjuna remains standing in the midst of an all-out battle, and his vision will be substantially colored by this. The distress he is about to endure is in part due to the martial setting. A poet sitting calmly by a secluded stream on a summer's day would have a vastly different interpretation than what Arjuna is about to expound.

Because of the "bad vibes" in the set and setting, Arjuna is beginning to have a paranoid reaction to his vision. We react negatively to the extent we are attached to a static image of ourselves. This is adroitly expressed by Carl Jung:

> If we try to extract the common and essential factors from the almost inexhaustible variety of individual problems found in the period of youth, we meet in all cases with one particular feature: a more or less patent clinging to the childhood level of consciousness, a resistance to the fateful forces in and around us which would involve us in the world. Something in us wishes to remain a child, to be unconscious or, at most, conscious only of the ego; to reject everything strange, or else subject it to our will; to do nothing, or else indulge our own craving for pleasure or power. In all this there is something of the inertia of matter; it is a persistence in the previous state whose range of consciousness is smaller, narrower, and more egoistic than that of the dualistic phase. For here the individual is faced with the necessity of recognising and accepting what is different and strange as a part of his own life, as a kind of "also-I."[14]

Many people enter spiritual life not in a dispassionate search for truth or scientific understanding but to make their fragile and defensive egos unassailable. By joining an established religious setup they become angelic by association, and any criticism of them can be taken as hostility toward God or the founding saint and dismissed out of hand. The implication is, "I'm in a divine gathering, which makes me divine too. Therefore if you disagree with me, you should be exiled or destroyed." We see this bald-faced egoism plainly in the two-year-old, but by adulthood the urge has been cloaked in more subtle—and potentially more deadly—guises. Adults' aggressiveness is clearly a defensive ploy, but unless they are convinced to drop it they will remain as they are.

Timid seekers cannot abide a guru who criticizes them. They seek the benignly smiling ones who treat them as their own dear child, or the pseudo-gurus whose anger is always hurled at others, and that's undoubtedly good enough for some. Shelter from the storm is adequate, and it satisfies the animal instinct to hide from danger. But brave seekers of truth like Arjuna must be prepared to undergo a baptism by fire, where the guru brings their faults out into the open so that they can be acknowledged and relinquished. Coming out of hiding, they eventually discover that there is nothing to fear, and they make strides toward genuine fearlessness.

Anyone embarking on a psychedelic trip for personal growth and insight should be prepared for a similar rude awakening. As the word *guru* means literally a "remover of darkness," whatever removes your darkness is a guru to you. It would be very unwise to take a psychoactive medicine with the idea that it is only going to stroke your ego and enhance your comfort zone. What you will learn is where your blockages are, your hidden crutches and defenses. If you aren't willing to give those up, tripping is not a good idea for you.

A "bad trip" is generally one where suppressed material from the unconscious surfaces to confront the conscious mind. Since we suppress precisely what we fear most, when it bursts out it can be exquisitely terrifying. Afterward, though, the one who has let it out may well find it has lost its sting and its power to manipulate.

Of course, it's possible that the soma brew of ancient India contained more toxic alkaloids than modern pharmaceutically pure psychedelics do, and these can definitely cause physical suffering that in turn makes a trip much more frightening than it would be otherwise. It is easy to imagine you are dying, for instance, when you are feeling powerful abdominal cramps. If your mind focuses on a bodily ailment while tripping, it can quickly magnify the problem to a major panic attack. Toxic alkaloids might be a factor in Arjuna's state of mind, but the Gita is concerned with presenting psychological truths rather than cataloguing all the effects mushrooms can have, so we may safely leave that question up in the air.

ON SEEING YOU TOUCHING THE SKY, SHINING IN MANY A COLOR, WITH MOUTHS WIDE OPEN, WITH LARGE FIERY EYES, MY INMOST SELF INTENSELY DISTRESSED, I FIND NEITHER COURAGE NOR CONTROL, O ALL-PERVADING ONE.

The dark side of our mental makeup often remains out of sight, fortunately for our stability, but a spiritual or psychedelic thrust will sooner or later unearth something ghastly that can blow away the meager defenses our complacency previously provided. When that happens, a sound philosophy can only offer a straw for the drowning one to grasp; it can't turn back the tide. There is nothing for it but to be bowled over. But the terror does not destroy; it tempers the mettle of the psyche and strengthens it.

The ego is very clever to take in all manner of spiritual teachings and subject them to its domination, and the resulting spiritual ego is extremely hard to dislodge from its perch. In the manner of an insular cabal excluding all non-believers, doubts and challenges are dismissed without a hearing. If we are particularly blessed, we may encounter an experience that floods the ego out of its ability to co-opt every lesson to its own self-glorification. Regardless of how it comes about, whatever produces the flood should be treated as our guru, the remover of our darkness. That's not so easy when our first instinct is to reject it.

This is an arena where psychedelics are particularly efficacious. They confront false beliefs, no matter how entrenched, with an irrefutable counterproposition. In the case of a human guru, it is always possible to retain a degree of ego as a buffer against the intensity imparted, but a unique ability of soma-type medicines is to temporarily circumvent all our conditionings. They can be reconstructed, and often are, but at least we are given an opportunity to choose between the valuable and the pernicious ones.

For a yogi, balance in all things is called for. A mere nod to life's negatives is not enough. Since we are blessed to have so much positivity most of the time, it is only right that this be counterbalanced in a way that cannot be denied. It may be that the terror is so intense because it equates with a vast amount of good times. And of course the exact proportions vary with every person. Ultimately, the intense direct experience of good and bad eventualities can be unified by the yogi to achieve a blissful neutrality that accepts and transcends both. It takes time.

In Jill Taylor's stroke account cited earlier, she indicates that most of our control, if not our courage, is located in the dominant, usually left, hemisphere of the brain. In her case a ruptured aneurysm took the place of the soma in opening her up to samadhi, taking her left brain offline and ushering her into conscious contact with previously hidden aspects of her self, those more in tune with what we call the absolute ground. She found the experience so delightful that she often wondered why she should bother to regain left-brain function at all. The distress many people feel in these circumstances comes from the left brain holding on as hard as it can to its fading dominance. It has a tough time admitting that there is a nonmanipulative part of our makeup, and an even tougher time surrendering to it. It uses fear as an octopus uses a jet of ink, as a smoke screen to hide behind. Once the urge to control is relinquished, though, we are able to relax and enjoy the ride.

HAVING SEEN YOUR MOUTHS FEARFUL WITH TEETH, LIKE TIME'S DEVOURING FLAMES, I LOSE MY SPATIAL BEARINGS AND FIND NO JOY; BE GRACIOUS, O LORD OF GODS, CONTAINER OF THE WORLD!

Here Arjuna has lost all sense of space and time and is entering a highly unsettling period of discontinuity. The ancient rishis apparently conceived of the world as a time/space continuum, just as we do.

Following up on Dr. Taylor's left and right brain analogy, spatial bearings, among others, are left-brain functions, while joy is a right-brain function. Arjuna is losing control of his whole mind now, not just half as with a stroke. The ultimate learning state only occurs when we rise out of ourselves completely. The transition is virtually the same as dying, and so it is resisted with whatever remains of a person's will to live, which is the source of the terror and distress. Even knowing the experience is temporary, as with soma ingestion, may not be adequate consolation. The fact is, anything that undermines the experience is going to make it less compelling than it could have been. The challenge is to surrender to all of it.

Losing one's bearings is what casts us into the transformative agony of direct experience, unmitigated by the fairytales we usually cushion ourselves with. Thomas Merton addresses an analogous stage of development in the opening paragraphs of *The New Man:*

Life and death are at war within us. As soon as we are born, we begin at the same time to live and die.

Even though we may not be even slightly aware of it, this battle of life and death goes on in us inexorably and without mercy. If by chance we become fully conscious of it, not only in our flesh and in our emotions but above all in our spirit, we find ourselves involved in a terrible wrestling, an *agonia* not of questions and answers, but of being and nothingness, spirit and void. In this most terrible of all wars, fought on the brink of infinite despair, we come gradually to realize that life is more than the reward for him who correctly guesses a secret and spiritual "answer" to which he smilingly remains committed. This is more than a matter of "finding peace of mind," or "settling religious problems."

Indeed, for the man who enters into the black depths of the *agonia,* religious problems become an unthinkable luxury. He has no time for such indulgences. He is fighting for his life. His being itself is a foundering ship, ready with each breath to plunge into nothingness and yet inexplicably remaining afloat on the void. Questions that have answers seem, at such a time, to be a cruel mockery of the helpless mind. Existence itself becomes an absurd question, like a Zen koan: and to find an answer to such a question is to be irrevocably lost. An absurd question can have only an absurd answer.

Religions do not, in fact, simply supply answers to questions. Or at least they do not confine themselves to this until they become degenerate. Salvation is more than the answer to a question.[15]

ALL THESE SONS OF
DHRITARASHTRA, WITH HOSTS OF
RULERS, BHISHMA, DRONA, AND
THAT SON OF A CHARIOTEER, WITH
OUR WARRIOR CHIEFS,

ARE RUSHING INTO YOUR FEARFUL
MOUTHS, TERRIBLE WITH TEETH;
SOME ARE FOUND STICKING IN THE
GAPS BETWEEN THE TEETH WITH
THEIR HEADS CRUSHED TO POWDER.

Verses 23 to 30 contain a subtheme of Krishna's mouth moving steadily closer to Arjuna, opening up and consuming everything on all sides of the battlefield he is standing on, and finally bursting into flames. Read together, the verses impart an intense sense of dread and horror that almost reaches off the page to grasp the reader by the throat. Back in the days when the tale was transmitted orally, we can imagine the guru acting it out, creeping slowly toward the disciples sitting cross-legged in the sand, then suddenly baring his teeth and scaring the pants (or dhotis) off them. It's hard to imagine a more hair-raising vision than what Vyasa has recorded.

The gristly mouth images symbolize how time eradicates everything, sooner or later. Arjuna is seeing the inevitability of death for all the seemingly stable figures in his life, most of whom surround him on the battlefield. Even for a hardened warrior this is a severe shock. Yet this kind of revelatory jolt is why soldiers sometimes feel more alive in combat than they ever do afterward. While we usually have some *idea* about death, the actual perception of it chastens us to the depths of our soul.

Arjuna is into the part of the trip where he would totally freak out if he hadn't entered it intentionally and consciously. Luckily he knows it is a vision induced by the potion his guru has given him, and that that worthy fellow is sitting right there acting as a lifeguard, so it is almost bearable. If he believed this mayhem just happened by accident, he might never be able to get over it. A soldier confronting death is sustained by patriotic fervor, while a yogi cast into the void is sustained by religious or philosophical imagery. None of it is a match for death, but at such a time we need all the help we can get.

The fear of death is an invisible motivator lurking within every pulsation of the world we live in. We can never be free of its influence until we acknowledge it out in the open. Krishna's vision brings death to Arjuna's attention hyperrealistically, so he can engage with the full measure of fear and horror it elicits.

Paradoxically, confronting death is an essential part of the true rebirth glibly preached but seldom practiced in many religions. Once you have experienced your own extinction, death loses its sting. You can at last go forward as a free human being who no longer has to choreograph your life to simply avoid pain and cling to islands of pleasure in a doomed sea of hostility.

Sanskrit famously uses the same word, *kala*, to indicate both "time" and "death." Time indubitably erases all traces of each life, sooner or later. In its inimitable way, death is about the most instructive guru of all. Arjuna is seeing this truth "up close and personal," with all its terrors unassuaged by being cloaked in well-worn concepts. He will soon beg for his favorite religious image to comfort him, but it will not appear.

The people mentioned here are all combatants in the war Arjuna is caught up in, letting us know that the setting is vehemently impinging on his state of mind. Again, this is an incidental aspect of the experience brought on by the environment, not necessarily an inevitable part of a spiritual vision.

A spiritual catharsis is seldom completely divorced from its context, even though there may be only occasional and tangential connection to the outside world. Arjuna's reference to the surrounding situation reminds us that the specific details of his vision are not universal but merely reflect his personal resonance with what's going on around him. We find a typical mixture of real and imaginary elements, similar to the dreaming state, as the mind provides symbolic adventures for real characters. Each visionary will understand and describe the Absolute based on their own mind-set and the setting in which their vision occurs. That doesn't make it right or wrong, only partial, less than absolute.

AS MANY RUSHING TORRENTS OF RIVERS RACE TOWARD THE OCEAN, SO DO THESE HEROES IN THE WORLD OF MEN ENTER YOUR FLAMING MOUTHS.

As if chewing everyone to bits wasn't bad enough, now the mouths have all caught fire, indicating a quantum intensification of Arjuna's trip. The furiously plunging rivers tell us that time has accelerated tremendously, a common effect of the ingestion of psychedelics. Time sense can be absent during the peak, as Arjuna experienced earlier, but as "normalcy" returns it may be distorted in any number of ways.

The course of life has often been compared to a river, seeping out of the ground in the remote, high mountains, following the course of its fate (in the form of gravity and topography) over and around many obstacles, joining forces with other similar streams, rushing headlong through the hills, before settling down to a more dignified existence in the lowlands as a carrier of traffic and enterprise. Ultimately it pours into the sea, symbolizing reunification with the Absolute. From the ocean, the vaporous spirit of water is lifted up to waft through the sky and return to the mountaintops as rain and snow, fulfilling the cycle again and again. Since he's quite agitated, Arjuna gives this poetic metaphor a hysterical slant. Soldiers on a battlefield rush headlong into death; there is no going gentle into any good night. The peaceful yogic merger with the ocean is elbowed aside by a mad dash to flaming extinction.

While this natural cycle of life and death is going on all the time, scenes of mass carnage make it seem as though the extinction aspect has somehow assumed a preeminent position. At the back of Arjuna's mind, he must be wondering, "We are all going to die soon enough. Why hurry the process? Can't we just stop for a moment?" Afterward he will be inspired to cherish every moment of life as if it were his last. Death, the great guru, can teach us how to truly live.

AS MOTHS SPEED INTO A BLAZING FIRE TO BE DESTROYED, JUST SO DO THESE WORLDS ALSO SPEED INTO YOUR MOUTHS UNTO THEIR DESTRUCTION.

This and the previous verse offer analogies for the battlefield setting. It looks like Arjuna is beginning to "come down" from the highest point, in which no comparison made sense. As his mind begins to gather itself back together, normal associative functions are gradually restored.

We cannot live forever in the white heat of unitive experience of the Absolute, at least in our current level of evolutionary development. Our mortal frame would be destroyed. We can only have a brief sip of the nectar of immortality and then strive to incorporate the expanded mentality it has imparted into our everyday life. A little goes a very long way, as Arjuna is realizing.

Moths are a perfect analogy for warriors, since they imagine they are doing the right thing by rushing to a flame, and yet they are plunging to their doom. Their duty as they see it is fatal, and yet they are eager for it. If you carry moths away from the fire they will fight you off and go right back to it.

I recall a similar insight that ended my brief stint in a university. During the Vietnam War, I visualized my academic career as being like a conveyor belt drawing me slowly but surely into the maw of the military/industrial complex, which then as always was bent on total and permanent warfare to appease its insatiable appetite. All of us in science and math were a lot like moths speeding toward the flames, as we eagerly competed for the best grades and the best schools, blinded by our naïveté and idealism. The conveyor belt vision did liberate me from that ill fate, as I dropped out and soon aligned myself with a guru of unsurpassed excellence, who helped me redirect myself to life-affirming choices. But plenty of other "moths" pressed ahead with high hopes, only to have their youthful idealism co-opted into gainful employment in the Death Star.

I have a young friend who recently graduated with an engineering degree and found a great job with a terrific salary building remote-controlled model airplanes. It was like being paid to play! Only gradually did it dawn on him that his "toys" were being used for the execution without trial of random people in faraway countries in an attempt to create enemies that could make the insanity of war seem legitimate. The lure of the flames is so strong that he is finding it hard to resist the good pay and seek more benign employment. The war machine is filled with good-hearted, trusting people like him who didn't bother to peek behind the curtain to see what was really going on.

Verse 30

YOU LICK UP ALL WORLDS,
DEVOURING ON EVERY SIDE WITH
YOUR FLAMING MOUTHS, FILLING
THE WHOLE WORLD WITH GLORY.
YOUR FIERCE RAYS ARE BLAZING
FORTH, O ALL-PERVADING ONE.

Arjuna's celestial vision ends with him imagining all life-forms on a high road to their destruction. It's as though they were born only so they could die. Again we can say, that's one way of looking at it, but surely their birth was the main point of the whole game in the first place?

Many people's trips end with a pervading sense of bliss and unity, which is perhaps a positive exaggeration. Like many others, Arjuna has ended his on a negative note, which is also an exaggeration. Any intense experience is likely to leave a person leaning one way or the other. So there is work to be done, to gather it all into a healthy, balanced perspective. With Krishna's help Arjuna will now get serious about his "postgraduate" studies: learning to be a fully free and independently motivated human being.

Because of his newfound conviction of the brevity of life, Arjuna will never again be oblivious of where he's going, like a heedless insect hurtling toward certain death. He will want very much to know what he should do with his hour on the stage to make it meaningful. The "glory" of simply being fuel for a funeral pyre isn't all that glorious when you have caught a whiff of the stench. Now he craves to know what the real point of life is and the best way to celebrate it.

It's a great paradox that a brush with death impels us to be more alive, and without its blessing we so often live as though we are already deceased. Several important people I have known stopped sleepwalking only when a doctor pronounced their death sentence from disease. The rude shock woke them right up, taught them what really mattered. Too bad they had so little time left to run with it. Yet another blessing of a psychedelic adventure is to remind us we are in a most temporary condition, and we must learn to be as alive as possible within the brief flicker of our moment in the sun.

TELL ME WHO YOU ARE, SO
FIERCE IN FORM! I BOW TO YOU,
O SUPERIOR GOD. BE GRACIOUS!
I WANT TO UNDERSTAND YOU,
O PRIMAL ONE, NOR DO
I KNOW YOUR POSITIVE
CONTINUED BECOMING.

The normal state of humanness is to identify with our beliefs, yet to not be aware of how thoroughly we do identify with them: "I am my ideas," "I am what I think," "I am what I have gone through," "I am my expectations," and so on. These might well be consciously denied but are deeply felt in the body. There's a lot of resistance in conjunction with letting go of such notions, if only temporarily. Arjuna's vision has completely smashed all such identifications. Now he wants to replace them with new ones, based more on conscious, neutral values than his former unexamined ones.

For the moment, though, Arjuna is undone by his experience. He knows somewhere in his memory that Krishna's final teaching was for him to become united with the Absolute in essence, devoted to the Absolute in intellect, sacrificial toward the Absolute in mind-set, and with an inward bow to That Alone in his every action. Freaking out, with his habitual outlook permanently superceded, all he can do is wildly claim that he is trying to bow—the very simplest of his options, but still more than he can handle—and beg for Krishna to explain to him what's going on. His last phrase, "I do not know your positive continued becoming," simply means, "I don't understand you." He might well add, "I don't understand anything anymore."

Nataraja Guru succinctly describes the impossibility of fully knowing the Absolute in his comments on this verse:

> The limit of the vision is reached in this verse in which it is only a mark of interrogation and exclamation that remains for Arjuna. The Absolute is still to be known. The vision only covers aspects of the Absolute, beginning from the ontological and leading up through the teleological to a notion that culminates in a tremendous mystery beyond which it is evidently impossible to reach through visions and descriptions. Arjuna is left in bewilderment even at the end of the most direct of visions that could possibly be described.[16]

At the end of a trip a person is in a highly suggestible state of mind. There is a new openness, coupled with a realization that there is a lot more going on than you once thought. It is important to be in the care of someone whom you trust to not lead you astray. This is the moment when a manipulative person could implant ideas at a deeper level even than hypnotic suggestion. Simple affirmations help gather your energy toward constructive vectors; paranoid or negative ones incite destructive behavior. Complete silence might foster a continuation of the confusion, or else it might permit some random thought to have an inordinate influence.

This is a particularly delicate moment in spiritual development, with the disciple susceptible to many kinds of input. A guru or guide must be very careful not to supply new identifications with a selfish or relativistic taint. The gist of the teaching is for us to live out a life in full awareness and harmony with the Absolute. In his response to Arjuna's plea, Krishna, as a guru par excellence, reiterates the call to arise spiritually and remain fully awake and alive. There is not a word about worshipping him or any other kind of groveling attitude. Likewise a therapist or guide will gently dissuade transference impulses in a patient whose gratitude is projected outward and focused on the messenger rather than the message.

KRISHNA SAID:

I AM WORLD-DESTROYING TIME,
GROWN INTO HARDENED MATURITY,
OPERATING HERE CONTINUOUSLY,
DESOLATING THE WORLDS.
EVEN WITHOUT YOU, NONE OF
THE WARRIORS STANDING IN THE
OPPOSING ARMIES SHALL CONTINUE
TO EXIST.

THEREFORE, ARISE AND GAIN FAME!
CONQUERING YOUR FOES, ENJOY
THE REALM OF ABUNDANCE.
BY ME THEY HAVE ALREADY BEEN
SLAIN. BE THE INCIDENTAL CAUSE
ONLY, ARJUNA.

DRONA AND BHISHMA,
JAYADRATHA, KARNA, AND THE

OTHER GREAT BATTLE HEROES,
ARE ALL SLAIN BY ME. DO NOT BE
DISTRESSED. FIGHT ON, YOU SHALL
CONQUER IN BATTLE YOUR RIVAL
CO-WARRIORS.

The opening phrase is what came into the mind of nuclear physicist Robert Oppenheimer as he witnessed the first atomic bomb test in 1945. The translation he himself made was "Now I am become death, the destroyer of worlds."[17] If he had had access to Sri Aurobindo's early twentieth-century version, it might have been even more apt as the gigantic mushroom cloud roared into the sky that morning: "I am the Time-Spirit, destroyer of the world, arisen huge-statured for the destruction of the nations."[18] As the same word in Sanskrit means "death" and "time," both translations are common, with time predominating in the more scholarly versions. On reflection, death and time are intimately related.

Like soma revealing the dormant power of consciousness, nuclear fission and fusion unleash a vast energy lying latent within matter. Energy and consciousness bear more than a passing similarity, and they could well be twin aspects of the same principle. The material universe is a transitory coalescence of virtually infinite energy, and its solidification as matter allows various types of beings to carve out a temporary existence in the face of those titanic forces. Beings are like islands of detritus that form on the surface of the ocean, only to be scattered again by the action of wind and waves. In the Vedantic viewpoint, consciousness coalesces as nature in a similar centripetal impulse. In either perspective, the ground of the seemingly ordinary is actually the unimaginably extraordinary.

Although we might be tempted to treat Krishna's destruction of the worlds or nations as drastic and negative, it is an integral part of the normal course of evolution. Not only that, but nations symbolize separateness, the more or less arbitrary boundaries imposed on a boundless world by human scheming. The perception of separation is considered by yogis to be a product of ignorance and the primary source of suffering, both individually and collectively. This being the case, when the Absolute eradicates separateness, it is not simply the end of a temporary paradigm, it is an affirmation of its underlying unity. Any form of temporal dissolution should be treated as just such an affirmation, which among other things will cause death to lose its hold over us.

Curiosity, which comes from the same root as *cure,* leads us to pry beneath the surface and reconnect with this supernal source. And while it is possible to proceed as if there is only a surface in life, seekers of truth are impelled by an unquenchable curiosity to hunt for their own cure through realization. While offering a sense of connection, of belonging and being "home" in a way, realization is also highly disconcerting, as the intensity of the energy released threatens to melt away whatever temporary forms have taken root on its face.

As in the attempt to harness atomic power, regaining conscious awareness of our origins is likewise fraught with danger. There is a lethal downside to counterbalance the ecstatic upside, and reintegrating the welter of new insights is both a challenge and an essential part of a meaningful existence. Without assistance, many fall by the wayside, permanently confused and disoriented by the experience. Like liberated atomic energy, the genie of expanded consciousness cannot easily be put back in the bottle. It will have to be intelligently taken into account in one's evolutionary development forever after.

It is important to see how these three verses are an answer to

Arjuna's plea of verse 31. He begs for Krishna to reveal who he is and explain his "positive continued becoming," which means his Time aspect with a capital T. In other words, what's going on and where is it all headed? Krishna's reply addresses his disciple's request measure for measure, in true guru fashion.

Arjuna first asked, "Tell me who you are," and Krishna replies, "I am Time." Arjuna then said, "I bow to you," and Krishna tells him to "arise and gain fame." When Arjuna says, "I don't understand you," Krishna responds that he, the Absolute, is the true cause of everything, whereas individuals are no more than incidental causes. He means there is a large-scale evolution taking place in the universe that is not subject to individual control, but within that grand scheme individuals do have a role to play in the unfoldment of their existence.

Commentators tend to take the imagery of these verses too literally, assuming that Krishna is directing Arjuna to rejoin the war and start fighting. Probably the widest-spread misconception surrounding the Gita is that it advocates war. Proponents of war conveniently ignore the frequent calls to ahimsa, non-hurting, and other gentle virtues, throughout the Gita.

The Gita has often been used to inflame warlike sentiments, and Arjuna does have his own actual war to wage—after all, he is a warrior standing on a battlefield. But the call to arise and fight here echoes Krishna's earlier demands that Arjuna stand up and face life. The primary exhortation of the Gita is for each of us to express ourselves to the best of our ability, to overcome our defects and live a full and meaningful life, in whatever manner best suits both us and our fellow beings.

The long history of Krishna's urging here is well worth recapitulating, so that we are less inclined to take it at face value. In chapter II, 37 and 38, Arjuna is asked to arise and fight with a neutral attitude to avoid sin, but Krishna also points out that this is the argument of rationalism and he has even better things up his sleeve. In verse 49 he says, "pitiful indeed are they who are benefit motivated," and acting to avoid sin is certainly an example of benefit-motivated action.

Even as near to the level of actual life as chapter III, verse 43, Krishna said, "Stabilizing the self by the Self, kill that enemy in the form of desire, so difficult to overcome." This means that what we have to combat is not an external enemy but our own ill-considered desires. As the Gita has become more idealized chapter by chapter, there is no reason to think that gross action is in any way being suddenly recommended now.

After III, 43, the next exhortation is IV, 42: "Therefore, sundering with the sword of Self-knowledge this ignorance-born doubt residing in the heart, stand firm in the unitive way, and stand up, Arjuna." Such a person "cannot be bound by works."

Chapter V concludes by saying the one who knows the Absolute in everything and as the friend of all beings reaches peace.

Chapter VI brings this trend to a peak in verse 5: "By the Self the Self must be upheld; the Self should not be let down; the Self indeed is its own dear relative; the Self indeed is the enemy of the Self." The chapter concludes in verse 46: "The yogi is greater than men of austerity, and he is thought to be greater than men of wisdom, and greater than men of works; therefore become a yogi, Arjuna." Fighting actual wars is the task of men of works. It would be quite out of keeping for Krishna to recommend it here in the eleventh chapter.

We should always keep in mind that Arjuna's foes are symbolic of inner challenges and are not simply men on a battlefield. The rest of us should be busy converting the symbolism to our own circumstances as they arise. Krishna's advice is true for every person in every situation. Superficially it sounds like an incitement to wage war, but it is in fact an invitation to live life to the hilt.

It is true, though, that Arjuna has found himself in the rare position of being a warrior in a legitimate war. "Legitimate wars" are rarer than dodos, but in this case Arjuna's family has plumbed every alternative, giving ground over and over. They have been left standing on a postage stamp–size plot of ground, and their foes are reaching to yank even that out from under them. When those conditions are truly met—and are not just hoped for in testosterone-fueled patriotic fantasies—actual fighting becomes a necessity.

In other words, self-defense after all else has failed is the sole legitimate excuse for warfare. Virtually all fighting on any scale is initially offensive, not defensive, though it is usually couched in propaganda to make it *seem* defensive, with the first offensive stroke being to blame the victim. The thirst for battle is clear evidence of mental instability; the fact that it is a widespread form of insanity does not legitimize it. One way of looking at yoga is that it is a method of becoming civilized, of rising above our base reactivity to respond with wisdom in place of violence; certainly it is the opposite of making war.

Modern warfare is a thousand times more terrible than in the relatively honorable days of the Gita. Then at least, war meant soldier versus soldier, fighting hand to hand. Now that civilians are prime targets, and the aim is to actually *create* an enemy by inflicting widespread misery and outrage among them, not to mention the total lack of contact between widely separated combatants, there is no possibility of honor in warfare.

Moreover, warriors in ancient India were *kshatriyas,* members of the second highest caste, with a lot of independence, not unlike medieval knights. Today all warriors below the highest rank are akin to *sudras,* the lowest, utterly servile caste. They are strictly prohibited from independent thought or action and so are merely glorified slaves, cannon fodder to be used as sacrificial pawns by policy makers.

The popular notion that the Gita is pro war is espoused particularly by those who harbor entrenched belligerent attitudes, who are looking for trouble. Such types always find a way to justify their behavior, including the invocation of divine sanction. The phrase "spoiling for a fight" is quite apt. When a person has been trained to retaliate aggressively against apparent provocations, the inner state is tilted toward hostility. Like a rotting fruit, the cancer starts innocently enough but soon spreads to destroy every bit of it. Again, as all spiritual teachers tell us, the inner state is the key. If you want peace you must be peaceful. If you are angry, you are constantly under stress and worse, and that will precipitate explosive situations.

The most acute problem from a spiritual perspective is that the typical human is predisposed to fight. It's not that we are neutral and simply answer the needs of the situation, but inwardly we are bristling for a confrontation. All sorts of apparent provocations are not true calls to battle but rather desperate cries for real solutions. As fighting has been venerated and practiced for millennia, there is a deeply lodged prejudice in its favor. If a yogi learns to act without predilections, the need to enter physical combat becomes extremely unlikely, though it cannot be utterly abandoned, as Arjuna's case indicates.

Moving along with our survey of Krishna's battlefield exhortations, chapter VII has no directive for Arjuna, and VIII speaks only of contemplatives in general, in verse 28: "Whatever meritorious result is found implied in the Vedas, in sacrifices, austerities and in gifts, the contemplative who is unitively established, having understood this (teaching), transcends all these and attains to the supreme primal state."

Chapter IX, verse 34, brings this ever-more-subtle sequence to a close with the teaching that sums up the highest conclusion of the Gita: "Become one with Me; be devoted to Me; sacrifice to Me; bow down to Me; unifying thus yourself, you shall surely come to Me, your supreme Goal none other than Me."

Remembering all this, when Krishna says we should conquer our foes, he is instructing us to overcome our obstacles, on every level. Arising to gain fame means becoming proficient in our chosen lifestyle. The fact that these obstacles or foes have already been killed by "Time" means that all our opposition will eventually vanish like the morning mist. Of course, so will we. An absolutist or scientific perspective sweeps away temporal difficulties, which are always manifested in the form of the people who embody them. Four specific people are mentioned here, who embody second-best characteristics in opposition to absolutism, namely magic and divine boons (Karna and Jayadratha), Vedic or religious ritualism (Drona), and well-meaning patriarchy (Bhishma).[19]

We can't ignore the implication that the flow of the Absolute through time is geared to sweeping away obstacles. The more we link up with its tidal surge, the easier it is to pass through life's many roadblocks. There is plenty of positive reinforcement in Krishna's words, especially the last part of verse 34, where he assures Arjuna he will prevail in his own battle. We should go forward in full confidence, and there is nothing like inner surety to enable it. But our confidence absolutely must be based on legitimate understanding, or it will too easily become the swaggering of inebriated souls marching toward disaster.

Noncontemplative people react to immediate influences and so find themselves eternally buffeted by necessity, but the contemplative eye is able to get "distance" on any situation. It is in this sense that the obstacles we face are all "killed" by Krishna as Time. We have to take the long view.

We might say that Arjuna's direct experience of the Absolute has accelerated him out of the highly pressurized here and now and into the everywhere and always. This marks his true birth as a philosopher or rishi. Typical of a guru, Krishna advises him at this very moment to also attend to the actual situation in which he finds himself. The task of the guru is to counterbalance any and all exaggerations of the disciple, so that between the two sides of the polarity absolute neutrality is preserved. If the disciple is captivated by trivial concerns, the guru will draw their attention to the big picture. If they are spaced out and unfocused, the guru gently (or rudely if necessary) brings them back to earth.

Imagine you have just had the most mind-blowing experience of your life, and you have barely begun to wonder what to make of it all. While sitting there totally bemused, your guide tells you to stop stewing and get on with your life, begin putting everything you've just learned into practice, suggesting that you can start by cleaning up your room and taking a bath. Then write about the experience you don't even understand yet. Isn't that just like a guru!

Arjuna is quite rightly undone by what he has been through. Without assistance he might very well lack direction and motivation and become entangled in side issues. Such has been the fate of many who traveled a similar road unaided. Like a medic at a disaster scene, Krishna steps in to administer first aid, to help drive away confusion and restore his patient to a positive role in keeping with his dharma. The Gita is supportive of healthy activity, here as ever.

The "realm of abundance" is this world, filled with everything we need for a challenging and fulfilling life. Krishna unequivocally instructs Arjuna to enjoy it and not to withdraw and retreat. We are here to make history a supremely interesting story, not a repetitive struggle with boredom.

We could try to imagine what other advice Krishna might have given at this critical juncture, and it would bring us to a better appreciation of Vyasa's choice. Should he say, "Okay now, let's tiptoe off the battlefield and seek refuge in a monastery, where we can spend our days in reflection"? Hardly. Krishna has always been trying to restore Arjuna to his true inner nature or dharma, and he has a very active temperament. Should he say, "Now that you've seen the truth, let's go establish a new life for you based on what you've learned"? Again, that might work if Arjuna were mired in a false livelihood, but the fact is that he *belongs* where he is. He really is a warrior. To have second thoughts about his life would be a waste of time, a manifestation of anxiety. He is an honorable person, already engaged in an honorable life. There's no reason for him to feel regret. So we find Krishna's advice very appropriate: "Stand up and fulfill the life you already have, imbued with your newfound wisdom." It's very beautiful. The actual battle will soon be over, but the challenges of life will never cease. Meeting them head on is the high road to happiness.

Verse 33 mentions Arjuna being an incidental cause only. This is similar to religious concepts of being an instrument of the divine, which has a dualistic timbre outside the parameters of unitive yoga. It is absolutely essential to recognize the voice in your head as your own ordinary descriptive chatter and not mistake it for divine instruction. Everyone has an inner narrator, but it is a sign of severe mental illness to unquestioningly or helplessly follow its dictates. Yoga is about transcending the mind's trivial chatter to access more substantive aspects of our being, not about becoming a raving lunatic driven by the voice of "God."

To understand this as good advice, we must recall the gist of Krishna's teachings to this point. The unmanifest cannot act; only manifested entities can act. We actualize unmanifest potentials as we live our lives. To listen to some imaginary voice inside and then try to follow its suggestions is a recipe for delusion and disaster, since that voice is merely a compendium of all that we have heard and thought and desired in our life. Something much more unitive is meant by these words, such as: "Don't take yourself so seriously! The world is evolving according to a vast unfolding drama, and you are but a gnat in the prevailing windstorm. So go ahead and frolic in the current, but please restrain yourself from unleashing your egotistical desires on the world around you. Don't get a swelled head and imagine you are running the show all by yourself. We are all in this together."

VERSE 35

SANJAYA SAID:
HAVING HEARD THAT SPEECH,
ARJUNA, STUTTERING EMOTIONALLY
AND TREMBLING WITH FEAR, WITH
PALMS JOINED WORSHIPFULLY,
BOWED DOWN BEFORE KRISHNA
AND SPOKE THESE WORDS:

Whatever Krishna said in the last three verses must have gotten through to Arjuna, based on his reaction. It was the ultimate answer to the ultimate question, and Arjuna is very appreciative. The words have satisfied him like nectar to one dying of thirst.

Arjuna now knows his interpretation of the Absolute as a person or even as a deity is inadequate. All limitations have fallen away, and he is inundated by a vision of Totality. His state is not conducive to returning to normal activity, at least not right away. Ideally he would instantly "arise and gain fame," but realistically a lot of work remains for him to normalize his consciousness. He needs to sort through his conditioned responses of neurological circuitry (*samskaras*) and discard the useless or outmoded ones, reinforcing instead the best of them. This is an ongoing activity. As Dr. Taylor puts it in her previously cited book:

> What most of us don't realize is that we are unconsciously making
> choices about how we respond all the time. It is so easy to get caught

up in the wiring of our preprogrammed reactivity (limbic system) that we live our lives cruising along on automatic pilot. I have learned that the more attention my higher cortical cells pay to what's going on inside my limbic system, the more say I have about what I am thinking and feeling. By paying attention to the choices my automatic circuitry is making, I own my own power and make more choices consciously. In the long run, I take responsibility for what I attract into my life.[20]

Aldous Huxley's theory of the brain as a reducing valve is relevant here. Similarly to quantum theory it holds that we select only a tiny percentage of the total sensory input with which to construct our worldview. Direct confrontation with the vastness of even the local universe is too much for anyone to deal with, so the brain blocks out nearly all of it, usually selecting one ensemble that either poses a threat or offers a possibility of reward. We become comfortable and even smug in our selected slice of world. If some event tears away the veils and allows in more of actuality than we can handle, the mind is blown, shocked into arrest, until it can wrap itself around the input. When the floodgates are opened and we are tossed into the maelstrom, we can only sink or swim. The rule to remember is that if you panic and flail you sink, but if you relax you float.

Arjuna is fortunate to have his guru present to help him deal with the oceanic experience he is just coming down from, since there is a very thin line (or no line at all) between a spiritual experience and insanity. Studies have shown that artistic creativity and schizophrenia overlap significantly, and an outmoded term for psychedelics, though still occasionally used, is psychotomimetics, drugs that mimic psychosis. Without assistance, some visionaries end up in the locked ward. In fact, the entire remainder of the Gita is designed to teach Arjuna how to integrate his experience so that he can cope with his heightened awareness and become a positive contributor instead of a misfit. Because rechanneling the unleashed creative energy of the mind can be inhibiting if overdone, the process must be handled with great insight and prudence.

VERSE 36

ARJUNA SAID:

O KRISHNA, IT IS BUT RIGHT THAT
THE WORLD IS DELIGHTED IN
PRAISING YOU, THAT DEMONS FLY
IN FEAR TO EVERY QUARTER, AND
THAT ALL HOSTS OF PERFECTED
ONES BOW IN ADORATION TO YOU.

Not only is Arjuna a little bit giddy, but he is more importantly demonstrating his newfound stature as a rishi-philosopher. Where before
he was asking innocent questions, he is now making incisive proclamations, asserting what he has just learned from his own experience. A
subtle but crucial threshold has been crossed, and Arjuna will never be
the same.

Nonetheless, we can't help but notice the dualism he inserts between
demons and perfected ones. Krishna has been uncompromisingly all-
inclusive throughout, insisting he is present everywhere, but Arjuna has
not yet risen to that rarified perspective. This may be the slight imper-
fection that leads to Krishna's excoriation of demonic types later on,
in chapter XVI. For now, we should realize that Arjuna's attitude isn't
completely "right," so we want to be careful not to adopt his "good guys
versus bad guys" mentality. Such mistakes have undermined many an
originally clear-eyed outlook. A seeker is granted a vision of the unitive

state, and afterward they may simplistically reason that the unitive view is right and the nonunitive is therefore wrong. Such an attitude eradicates the unity and almost unnoticed opens the door to all manner of conflicts. Krishna has been advising Arjuna all along to stand up for his place in the scheme of things with a unitive attitude, not as a self-righteous warrior. The distinction is subtle but crucial.

The most important lesson to take from this is that we may well feel enlightened and ready to make cogent proclamations after a trip, but it could be pure hubris as much as pearls of wisdom. We should be careful to observe ourselves closely and be prepared to hold back, so that our ego doesn't run away with us. Our newfound freedom should be directed more inward than outward, for a number of reasons. It keeps us from raving, and it reminds us that other people have not shared our experience and don't necessarily want to hear about it. Our own psyche is the proper field for transformation and not so much the world outside, which has its own independent trajectory.

AND WHY SHOULD THEY NOT
BOW TO YOU, O GREAT SELF, MORE
VENERABLE EVEN THAN BRAHMA,
THE FIRST MAKER, O ENDLESS GOD
OF GODS, BASIS OF THE UNIVERSE!
YOU ARE THE IMPERISHABLE ONE,
EXISTENCE AND NONEXISTENCE, AND
WHAT IS BEYOND EVEN THAT.

Once upon a time, humanity grasped how intelligent the universe was. Every cloud and feature of the landscape was known to be alive, and every living creature was respected for its wisdom.

Then there followed an interim period where we adopted a hypothesis that only humans were intelligent, and all else was inert, blind, or otherwise stupid. This permitted rampant exploitation of the planet and its creatures, but it otherwise was an utterly bankrupt theory, not to mention criminal and in the long run possibly even suicidal. The list of cruelties inflicted by the human race on its fellow beings is an endless litany of horror. Thankfully, we are slowly regaining an appreciation of just how amazing the universe truly is and how intelligent all its parts are. Not just animals, with their demonstrably similar kinds of intelligence to humans, but plants, single cells, and even atoms and molecules, are coming to be known as aware of and interactive with their environment. Mimi Guarneri, a respected cardiologist, has even presented scientific evidence that the human heart has an intelligence of its own, independent of the brain, located in its own nerve ganglion.[21] Planetary and even larger systems are beginning to be seen as functioning intelligently by some measures. So the tragic—stupendously tragic—conceit of the human race is easing up a little. Yogis should abet the process by cultivating humility and an appreciation of how wise the cosmos in fact is. We are not the most advanced intelligence around. We are unique in some ways, but we are dwarfed by the intelligence that keeps all systems in harmony and running virtually forever. The tiny bit we understand is bestowed on us by this all-encompassing principle of conscious intelligence, to which we should be eternally grateful, as Arjuna is to his favorite example of it, Krishna.

Mark Twain expressed a similar antihubris sentiment with devastating sarcasm in an essay titled "Was the World Made for Man?" in which he lampoons the pretension that evolution has its culmination in humanity. As the Creator struggled to bring about the human race:

> It was foreseen that man would have to have the oyster. Therefore the first preparation was made for the oyster. . . . This is not done in a day. . . . At last the first grand stage in the preparation of the world for man stands completed, the oyster is done. An oyster has hardly any more reasoning power than a scientist has; and so it is reasonably certain that this one jumped to the conclusion that the nineteen million years was a preparation for him; but that would be just like an oyster, which is the most conceited animal there is, except man. And anyway, this one could not know, at that early date, that he was only an incident in a scheme, and that there was some more to the scheme, yet.[22]

Of course, scientists have come a long way since Twain's time, but the all-too-human propensity to imagine we are the last word in evolutionary excellence is still quite persistent.

VERSE 38

YOU ARE THE FIRST OF THE GODS, AND THE ANCIENT SPIRIT; YOU ARE THE SUPREME BASIS OF THE UNIVERSE; YOU ARE BOTH THE KNOWER AND THE KNOWABLE; YOU ARE THE (TRANSCENDENT) BEYOND AND THE (IMMANENT) RECEPTACLE (HERE); THE UNIVERSE IS PERVADED BY YOU, O ONE OF LIMITLESS FORM!

Arjuna's philosophical outlook is improving rapidly as he attains some distance on his momentous visions, and this verse is much more unitive—if such a notion can be excused from being an oxymoron—than his previous attitudes. All the terms used here have appeared before, but now it is apparent that Arjuna truly understands what they mean. He is speaking declaratively, from his own direct knowledge. He has made them his own.

Arjuna's newly established excellence as a philosopher-yogi is evidenced in his dialectical pairing of some of the terms. Arjuna now knows that all the dualities of life are subsumed in the unity of the Absolute, which he addresses familiarly here as "You."

The first phrase of the verse unites the two main streams of religious thought in the Gita's time, the shining ones of the present and the ancestral legacy of the past. Even today religions and philosophies have two faces, one more mystical, concerned with immediate perception of reality, and the other expressed in the worship of traditional values, honoring formulas and symbols. There is no good reason that these cannot coexist and be mutually supportive, but partisans have a tendency to threaten each other and even initiate pogroms. Until we are solidly grounded in our own understanding, we often feel insecure about our beliefs when other people disagree with us or simply have different goals. Where religions are often pitted against each other, Arjuna now sees them as different aspects of a single underlying truth.

Individuals evince the same dichotomy. We have moments of direct involvement with the here and now, interspersed with long periods when we glide along almost ritualistically, relying on memory and habit. Intelligently integrating both capacities makes for expertise in daily life.

"Knower and knowable" clearly belong together as a matched pair; their synthesis is knowledge. The keynote of Vedantic philosophy is that the knower and what is known both arise together from a universal consciousness, and bringing them together restores the absolute basis of awareness.

The word translated as "Receptacle" (*dhama*) has elsewhere been called the "Supreme Abode," meaning the all-encompassing unmanifest in which all of manifestation resides, or into which it is periodically received back. Nataraja Guru is correct to perceive that since the transcendent and immanent aspects are being paired here, the word is used specifically to imply immanence, a relationship with the natural world. This is yet another of the essential paradoxes addressed in Vedanta, and uniting them is a supreme achievement.

Even "Limitless Form" is a dialectical pair. Form has to be limited or it makes no sense, and what is unlimited cannot be constrained in any form. Yet when these are combined, the incomprehensible Absolute emerges from the paradox.

A common aftereffect of the psychedelic experience is a proclivity for seeing the contrary of every proposition. Immediate awareness of the flip side of everything leaps to mind instantaneously. Because it is the true nature of the cosmos, the unity underlying duality is readily accessed as soon as the mind is able to let go of its one-sided prejudices. It is not a state that has to be built up from piecemeal ideas but one that is only revealed.

Once unity has been apprehended, it is seen everywhere. The knack for perceiving it tends to "wear off" as the dual function of the left brain wakes back up, and that's fine for dealing with everyday routines. In a dualistic universe unity is often "out of place," and it can even render a person dysfunctional. But the ability to access a nondual state of mind is very valuable for our inner well-being, and it can be retained with practice. Recognizing the unity of life is a mark of adulthood, which explains why many early societies used psychedelic medicines as a rite of passage. Children cling to their partial understanding, fearful of letting go of it because the Beyond is unknown to them. They become adults when they learn to trust what the universe has to offer beyond threats to their survival.

You are the God of Wind, Death, Fire, Ocean, the Moon, first of Progenitors and the Great-Grandsire. Hail! Hail to You! A thousand times and again, hail! Hail to You!

If we borrow earth from the previous verse in the guise of the "Supreme Basis," we once again discover all the great elements here, connected as they are with the seven chakras or energy centers of the body. Chakras are mystical points connecting the individual with the cosmos, and as such they are used in many types of meditation. Briefly, the first chakra is located at the tip of the spine, the second near the genitals, the third in the solar plexus, the fourth in the heart, fifth in the larynx, sixth between the eyebrows (the infamous third eye), and seventh at the fontanels, the "soft spot" at the top of the skull. One of the Gita's techniques is to secretly weave these into Krishna's discourse, as is done here.

"Form" (Basis), "Ocean," "Fire," and "Wind" are related to the first four chakras, more commonly called earth, water, fire, and air. "Death" must be associated with the fifth chakra, that of *akasha,* or space. Death allows life to exist just as space allows matter to exist, by "making room" for it. The "Moon" is ever a symbol of individual consciousness, since it is a reflection of the light of the Source, the sun, and so is located in the sixth chakra. True origination pours in through the seventh chakra, which is thus the "first of Progenitors."

Reading between the lines, Arjuna's meditation as he regains awareness of his body is to tune in to each chakra in turn and connect it with the Absolute in principle, thereby harmonizing his entire system and flooding it with energy. This is an excellent meditation any time, but is especially effective in his expanded state of mind.

The most important lesson in this is that Arjuna is realizing nontheoretically that Krishna is the Absolute, which means he is Everything. If Arjuna were to become merely a literal Krishna worshipper, he would be limiting his idea of the Absolute to a specific form. But he knows he must love everything equally, because everything is equally infused with divinity. Several times already the equality of everything has been underlined by Krishna, most notably in V, 18, and VI, 8 and 9. For instance, the last of these reads, "As between dear well-wishers, friends, enemies, those indifferent, those in-between, haters, relations, and also as between good people and sinners, he who can maintain an equal attitude, excels."

PROSTRATIONS TO YOU BEFORE
AND AFTER; PROSTRATIONS TO YOU
ON EVERY SIDE; O ALL, OF ENDLESS
POTENCY AND IMMEASURABLE
STRENGTH, YOU TERMINATE ALL,
THEN YOU BECOME ALL!

Another series of dialectical statements epitomize Arjuna's newfound insights. He is exploding with joyful amazement as he discovers how everything fits together so symmetrically to produce a perfect universe, and it forces him to bow his head in awe. Krishna has asked him to remain standing, so it is a mental obeisance, an inward gesture of appreciation, not a physical one.

Arjuna first prostrates to both time and space, or in other words, to all vertical and horizontal factors in the scheme of things. He is expanding beyond the here and now of his immediate vision to begin to take the past and the future into account ("before and after") as well as the vast extension of the material universe ("on every side"). "Potency and strength" together are a matched pair, as in potential and kinetic energy. Every actualization reveals a formerly hidden potential and unleashes its forces, and realizing this will imbue Arjuna with an eagerness to express his own latent talents. The third pair is destruction and creation, expressed as "termination and becoming." Krishna as the

Hindu Vishnu is assigned the role of preserver in between those two poles, but Arjuna now recognizes that the Absolute comprises all three aspects of existence at once: everything comes into being, lasts a little while, and then disappears.

Most other commentators render the last phrase along the lines of "You permeate all, then you become all," which is basically redundant. Because he understands the secret of yoga as taught by the Gita, Nataraja Guru calls on a different sense of the Sanskrit original: "to finish, bring to a conclusion or put an end to," even simply, "to destroy." Translating it this way tells us that Arjuna now understands the cyclic nature of the universe and the Absolute's role in it. During his trip, Arjuna became so mesmerized by the destructive aspect of the Absolute that he couldn't see past it. Now he is confident that creation, preservation, and destruction operate eternally in rotation. Coming into existence and going out of it are mirror images floating on a sea of eternity.

At this stage, when Arjuna is emerging from his vision and gathering himself together filled with new vistas, everything has taken on a more profound significance than he ever knew in his former semi-alert state. At the same time, he is about to realize that he previously treated Krishna as his servant, and before that his friend, and now he feels mortified about his radical underestimation of who his guru really is. His new, heightened awareness will lead him naturally to the self-deprecating embarrassment over his former lack of respect that is expressed in the next pair of verses.

It is really disconcerting if we become aware of the baseline of arrogance that many of us adopt as a matter of course to survive in a seemingly hostile world. If we realized how callous and heedless we are of the manifold wonders of existence, it would be like suddenly standing naked in front of a crowd, or in the eyes of God, as it is sometimes poetically put.

I vividly recall a similar exposure in my own life, in 1971, when Guru Nitya wrote to all of us living with him in the newly founded Portland Gurukula that "there is an assumed superiority in the mind of all the aggressive races who have built up their fortune on the unwilling meekness of slaves. There is a concealed cruelty right in the heart of all their enthusiasm and kindness. As I see this ugly face sometimes very pronounced behind their sweetness and sincerity, I cannot help pointing my finger at it."[23] He was speaking partly about himself as a dark-skinned Indian, and how we were taking him for granted and showing very little appreciation for all he was doing for us. We were a bunch of white, very fortunate youngsters who were essentially clueless, and we did assume that it was our birthright to be catered to by even a great guru. Nitya's barb caused me intense pain and shame, and it prodded me to closely reexamine how I saw myself in relation to people from different backgrounds.

Arrogance is the flip side of deference. Krishna's call to Arjuna to stand up means not to either grovel or swagger but to achieve a normalized awareness and neutrality about his environs. He will first have to lose all vestiges of his princely conceit, both conscious and unconscious, before he can attain that expert balance.

WHATEVER I HAVE SAID RASHLY,
FROM CARELESSNESS OR FONDNESS,
ADDRESSING YOU AS "O KRISHNA,
O YADAVA, O COMRADE," THINKING
OF YOU AS AN INTIMATE AND
IGNORANT OF YOUR GREATNESS,

AND FOR WHATEVER JESTING
IRREVERENCE I MAY HAVE SHOWN
YOU, WHETHER AT PLAY, REPOSING OR
SEATED, OR AT MEALS, EITHER WHEN
REMAINING BY MYSELF OR WHEN
YOU WERE PRESENT, THAT I ASK YOU
TO FORGIVE, O UNPREDICABLE ONE!

We knew this was coming: Arjuna now feels keen embarrassment over having mistaken the paradisiacal nature of everything for some sort of "ordinary" reality. We all do this as a matter of course, so it's nothing peculiar to him. We treat the miracle of existence as if it were nothing more than a trivial accident. We imagine the mind is merely an epiphenomenon of matter, as though matter itself is something dead and inert! Einstein demonstrated that matter is merely a temporary form of nearly infinite energy, and it's really only an *appearance* of form at that. Scientists take for granted that every atom within matter is a whirling swirl of intensely focused activity, and yet at some point in processing that truth there is a disconnect. When we conceptualize something, it tends to become inert, static, fixed in time and space. The fault lies not in the material universe itself but in our way of looking at it.

Arjuna has just had his own concepts explosively revised to reveal what he, like Hamlet's Horatio, has been leaving out of his philosophy. Misunderstanding leads to conflict that may well escalate to full-on warfare, leaving the participants exhausted and impoverished and wondering how to avoid ever doing *that* again. As this has happened time and time again throughout history, it seems that more people would be inclined to reexamine their assumptions with an open mind in advance, but apparently it is a difficult exercise, best facilitated by some kind of shock. After all, "the darkness around us is deep," as the poet William Stafford puts it.[24]

Early learning programs are aimed at fixing a workable picture of reality so that the developing child can safely function. There is a tremendous sense of accomplishment in operating the body and in becoming an integrated member of the local tribe. As we grow up, most of us either rest in our satisfaction over fitting in or else sulk about the fact that we don't. Only the seekers, the few who dare to aim at transcendence of the status quo, look beyond the ordinary. But no one can fully prepare for a leap into totality. At that moment everything is renewed. What was dead becomes filled with life, and what was taken for granted can never be fully subscribed to again. The universe is known to be dynamic, ever changing. The seer can only bow in amazement at the wonder of it all. Arjuna also feels the unique pleasure of realizing the profundity of his blindness as it falls away. It seemed so right, and all of a sudden it looks ridiculous! The awareness is humbling, and it helps reduce the ego, which otherwise can blunder into a messianic complex when it is granted an extraordinary vision. People who undergo this transformative experience will almost certainly regret the entrenched attitudes they formerly clung to, but those attachments should be relinquished with a minimum of fuss. Here, Krishna will certainly forgive Arjuna his unintentional ignorance, because the game of life is all about shedding ignorance in favor of wisdom.

It is not uncommon for the beneficiaries of psychedelic experience to be elated by what feels like divine love and insight and later to be chagrined at how swaggering and ignorant all their former attitudes were. We act as if we know what we're doing, when in fact we know virtually nothing. Our certitudes are merely habitual assumptions and defensive barricades. If we examine our former attitudes while in an elevated state, they seem aggressive and boorish, as well as incredibly egotistical. They weigh us down, pin us to the ground. Trip or no trip, Arjuna has just arrived at this same embarrassing realization. The great thirteenth-century commentator of the Gita, Dnyaneshwar Maharaj, paraphrases how Arjuna feels.

I bow to everything whether it has form or not, because You dwell in it. Again and again, O Lord of the world, I bow to you. . . . Dwelling in the heart of every one, you pervade everything. . . . Therefore, You are near every one at all times. You are All. I have been stupid, and, not knowing this greatness of Yours, have treated You with familiarity. I have used nectar for washing the floor. . . . I found a mountain of precious stones, but broke them up, to prepare a parapet, and I used the wood of the most valuable tree to make a fencing round my farm. I have wasted my intimacy with You, O Krishna, for worthless objects. Even to-day in this mundane warfare, I have made You, Who are the embodiment of Para Brahma, my charioteer. . . . O Lord of the world, we have used you for our petty purposes. You are the final goal of the Samadhi, which Yogis are trying to reach, and yet I have behaved badly. You are the origin of the universe, and yet I crack jokes with You. When I came to Your palace and You omitted the usual formalities, I was upset. I have taken liberties with You. I have turned my back on You. I have challenged You to a wrestling bout. I have fallen out with You over a game of chess. I have asked You to give me valuable things. I even tried to instruct You, though You are all-knowing. The extent of my faults knows no bounds. With my hands on Your feet . . . I now declare that I did all this through ignorance. To Your invitations I demurred through pride. . . . The rivers collect dirty water and move toward the ocean, but the ocean receives them all the same. . . .

Save me from my errors, O Lord. I did not realize that You were the benefactor of the world. I even resented such respect being paid to You. You have allowed me to be praised in assemblies, when all the praises should go to You. I have spoken of You carelessly in the past. I have done this through ignorance and error, and now I turn to You for being saved.[25]

The passage displays the kind of sincere realization that sweeps outmoded attitudes aside and paves the way for clearer thinking. We can see here a prefiguring of ecological awareness, too, centuries ahead of the crowd.

As to the uncommon epithet "O Unpredicable One," the falsity of predication is a concept found in the philosophy of Narayana Guru, along with a small number of earlier philosophers. Verses 41 and 42 of his *One Hundred Verses of Self-Instruction* deal with it specifically, and his disciple Nataraja Guru expanded the idea in much of his work. Briefly, in the sentence "This is a pot," "This" is the subject and "pot" is the predicate. Under examination the This turns out to be highly mysterious, like the Absolute itself. We only know what This is when we define it with a predicate such as pot. Pot satisfies us because it is a specific thing we can recognize. We live in a world of predications of the mysterious This, and we content ourselves with just the predicates. We don't bother looking for the subject, the This. Here Arjuna recognizes the Absolute as "unpredicable," meaning it can't be adequately defined by any predication, any definition. In fact it would be absurd to even try, though of course humans love nothing better than to make more or less honorable attempts to pin it down.

The word Nataraja Guru translates as "unpredicable," *aprameya,* means "immeasurable, unlimited, unfathomable; not to be proved."

Even more interesting, it is the negation of *prameya,* which is "that of which a correct notion should be formed, an object of certain knowledge, the thing to be proved or the subject to be discussed."[26] In other words, if we form a correct notion of the Absolute it is no longer the Absolute. If we are certain about it we are certainly deluded. It does not require proof and is impossible to prove anyway, so perhaps it shouldn't even be talked about. We definitely should not strut around brimming with confidence that our particular predication is the only right one, cocksure it exceeds everyone else's and spoiling for a fight to prove it.

YOU ARE THE FATHER OF THE
WORLD, OF THE MOVING AND
UNMOVING; YOU ARE TO BE
REVERENCED BY THIS WORLD, AND
ARE THE SUPREME GURU; NONE IS
YOUR EQUAL; HOW THEN COULD
THERE BE ONE GREATER THAN YOU,
EVEN IN THE THREE WORLDS,
O ONE OF INCOMPARABLE
GREATNESS!

A reverential attitude is the best insurance against developing a bloated ego from the kind of transcendental experience Arjuna has just undergone. Throughout the Gita the arrow of interest and devotion is turned away from the ego toward the Absolute, which helps minimize the coloration of imaginary beliefs that so often confuse the seeker of truth. Krishna began the instruction by trying to pry Arjuna out of his socially indoctrinated mind-set, but there is always a significant remnant no matter how thorough the training, as the next verse will demonstrate. It is supremely difficult to distinguish between valid experience and ego-tainted experience. Since the disciple cannot attain self-awareness without a measure of prejudice, the assistance of a guru or therapist is essential.

Reflecting a similar reverential attitude, Narayana Guru wrote, in his mystical poem *Svanubhavagiti,* verse 33:

> *Oh Gracious Lord, your sportive game is*
> *revealed to me by your Grace.*
> *And that revelation is a precious scripture to me.*
> *The blessedness of your Grace flanked on either*
> *side by darkness and light—*
> *Oh Meaning of Meaning dancing in my heart.*

And verse 63:

> *Not knowing who the master is,*
> *oh my Lord, seeking you, so many here,*
> *having lost their wits,*
> *go astray, confused with their*
> *confounding reason.*[27]

Those who only hear half the message tend to become exclusive and possessive about their concepts of the Absolute. Bookstores bulge with pretentious tomes proclaiming this or that certitude, which will be obsolete by next season. Half-baked thinkers insist on grilling people about their beliefs, probing for disqualifying ideas and sneering at perceived weaknesses, in the desperate hope that by denigrating others they are somehow elevating themselves. But Krishna has made it abundantly clear that our beliefs and even our actions are wholly irrelevant. They are impediments to realization, not catalysts for it. By abasing the other you abase yourself, and vice versa. The projection of latent self-hatred in the form of an urge to repress others leads to all levels of conflict, up to and including "holy" war.

It is a great blessing to realize our limitations and learn humility, as Arjuna is now doing. A life of bombast is constrictive and binding, after all is said and done, and it is likely a mask for deep insecurities. Spiritual evolution is much gentler and more peaceful, and it is not afraid to include compassion and support for others. This reveals yet another paradox: that by accepting our faults we grow stronger, but by flaunting our strengths we undermine ourselves.

THEREFORE BOWING DOWN AND
PROSTRATING MY BODY, I SEEK
YOUR GRACE, O ADORABLE LORD;
(IT IS BUT PROPER THAT) YOU
SHOULD BEAR WITH ME, AS FATHER
TO SON, AS FRIEND TO FRIEND,
AS LOVER TO BELOVED.

Even Krishna is not capable of preventing Arjuna from lying down at
his feet, no matter how often he has insisted that he stand up. Some
cultural habits are too deeply engrained for even a god to overcome! As
the German polymath Friedrich Schiller wryly put it, "Against stupidity
even the Gods struggle in vain."

But Arjuna isn't really stupid, only sincerely chastened, and his
prostration symbolically counteracts his former egotism. Just this once
it has a role to play. Ritualistically continued, it would turn into just
another tool of the ego to prove his holiness, but that is not his intent.

Throughout this section Arjuna is rapidly surrendering his exaggerated sense of self in exchange for an open and guileless state that
is much more amenable to a spiritual lightness of being. Like a snake
shedding its skin, he is discarding his old attitudes, making room for
a much more expansive person. He is seeing clearly how his previous
attitudes were like prisons in which he languished, and he is renouncing

them one by one. As Socrates well knew, penetrating self-examination is crucial to making our life worth living.

The realization that energizes a serious reassessment of our lives is that each of us is little more than a dust mote in an infinite cosmos, and no human or group of humans has more than a slim grasp on the full implications of that cosmos. Spiritual striving certainly broadens our amplitude, but there is a real danger when merging into the Absolute that the individual retains a sense of self that is then expanded beyond all sensible limits. Individual empowerment acquired through spiritual effort can lead to megalomania or spiritual egotism if it is not counter-balanced with a commensurate humility.

The vision he has had has put Arjuna in his place as a mere speck in a vast incomprehensible maelstrom. Being aware of his finitude, he is less likely to get a swelled head. This teaches us that it is a valuable tool to continue to think of the Absolute as being more than we are, even when theoretically there is no difference. Whatever we do as individuals, without exception, is limited. While retaining our individuality we can only merge in an abstract sense, and if we were truly merged our individuality, centered in the ego, would not be functional for the duration of the experience.

It is of more than passing interest that Arjuna lists three archetypal, dialectical relationships that define his discipleship with Krishna. They can be thought of as those between parent and child, between friends, and between lovers, all of which are made out to be aspects of a guru-disciple bond. Arjuna continues to employ his dialectical wisdom here, expressing each of the three as matched pairs. The first indicates the profound respect and deference accorded to a guru early in the approach, not unlike a child deferring to their primary caregiver, especially one where the respect is tinged with fear, as is often the case with fathers. And, like a parent, the guru is equally interested in fostering the maturation of the disciple under their care. This somewhat guarded relationship progresses to mutual respect and a more equal status as it blossoms into friendship. The culmination occurs with the dissolution in unity of the apparent separation of guru and disciple, which Arjuna compares to two lovers merging into a single soul.

Pictorially, the first pair represents a vertical polarity, the second a horizontal polarity, and the third a perfect integration of them, like the point of intersection of the two axes. Yoga is the gathering together of horizontal and vertical factors into oneness.

Many seekers, who would rather remain circumspect than bare their souls, are content to maintain a more distant pose and so remain at the first stage, which insulates them from the fearsome possibilities a guru represents. Seekers who are very fortunate might progress to a genuine friendship with their guru, which offers many more possibilities for personal growth. Only a few go beyond friendship to enter the true mind-meld of spiritual lovers. Arjuna has now experienced all three stages, and he is wide open to receive the wisdom that Krishna will now begin to transmit to him, heart to heart. In a very few words the Gita has outlined one of the most profound and important relationships humans are capable of.

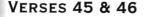

VERSES 45 & 46

I AM GLAD HAVING SEEN WHAT HAS NEVER BEEN SEEN BY ANYONE BEFORE, AND MY MIND IS TROUBLED WITH FEAR; O GOD, BE PLEASED TO SHOW ME THAT VERY FORM, O GOD OF GODS, O ABODE OF THE UNIVERSE;

I WANT TO SEE YOU EVEN SO, DIADEMMED, WITH MACE AND DISCUS IN YOUR HAND; ASSUME THAT VERY FORM WITH FOUR ARMS, O THOUSAND-ARMED, O ONE OF UNIVERSAL FORM!

Untethered, our psyches may plunge into a total, unimaginable vision. There are no words linked with memories to describe the immediacy of it. The tsunami of life sweeping from birth to death in a tremendous tide arrests our everyday mind in amazement. The Absolute is the Forbidden Territory that only the brave or the foolish dare to enter (three cheers for fools!). Society has warned us against trying to gain

143

admittance. Even a great warrior like Arjuna becomes terrified on the doorstep, the fear momentarily outweighing all conscious assessment of the beneficence and beauty beyond the portal.

Whatever sense of self we retain shrinks back from the black hole of the void at the center of our personal galaxy, revealed in the vision of the Real. The operative emotion is stark terror. Since we take our life thoroughly for granted, and have been spoon-fed endless sweet fairy tales about where it is headed, it is a serious shock when our individuality appears to be on the verge of extinction.

Stunned, Arjuna is now begging to be returned to the more or less conventional image of the god Vishnu with which he began his trip, so he can pigeonhole his experience and be soothed by something he can easily comprehend. When he begs Krishna to show him a familiar form that he can latch on to, the vision comes to a close. There is no going back and no standing pat either. It is not uncommon to want to hold on to the glories of a psychedelic excursion, but as the medicine wears off they fade away like dew before the sun.

It is important to notice that Krishna does not honor Arjuna's request, and he doesn't even go so far as to acknowledge it. This is a powerful symbolic gesture with many implications, well worth pondering. A few of its meanings are: clinging to religious iconography (often called idolatry) is antithetical to a spiritual state of mind, because our inclinations are to interpret new experiences in familiar terms, but that deadens them; Vishnu is himself a symbol of something without form, and he thus is only a poetic image; Arjuna's desire is a sign of weakness in someone who is now supposed to be strong enough to stand on his own two feet; we should always take things as they are and not long for something "other." Clearly, worlds are communicated by Krishna ignoring Arjuna's plea.

In *Memories, Dreams, Reflections,* Carl Jung writes of his own near-death experience and the outgrowths of it, which are remarkably like Arjuna's experience in meaning if not in shape. Time is an important factor in both visions, with the compression of past, present, and future into the now. It is accompanied by an oceanic "high" in which the detritus of life is painfully stripped away. Arjuna begs for the reinstatement of his individuality, but Jung was eager to be rid of it, as he could see how it had hampered him. He reluctantly reentered his body only because his doctor came to him in the vision as he was heading for the exit and brought him back. Jung sensed that this would mean the doctor would have to die in his place, and in fact, the day Jung left his sickbed, the doctor entered his own and never left it.

What Jung learned from "leaving his body" parallels many of the Gita's teachings, and when a similar conclusion is reached from two very different approaches, it lends weight to them. Jung shares with Arjuna the life-affirming insights that can be gained from venturing near death. As an example, Jung writes:

> Something else, too, came to me from my illness. I might formulate it as an affirmation of things as they are: an unconditional "yes" to that which is, without subjective protests—acceptance of the conditions of existence as I see them and understand them, acceptance of my own nature, as I happen to be [Vedantins would call it Jung's dharma]. At the beginning of the illness I had the feeling that there was something wrong with my attitude, and that I was to some extent responsible for the mishap. But when one follows the path of individuation, when one lives one's own life, one must take mistakes into the bargain; life would not be complete without them. There is no guarantee—not for a single moment—that we will not fall into error or stumble into deadly peril. We may think there is a sure road. But that would be the road of death. Then nothing happens any longer—at any rate, not the right things. Anyone who takes the sure road is as good as dead.[28]

The "sure road" is marked out by religious dogma and rigidly conventional beliefs, but to the extent that these diverge from reality they fail to protect us from the consequences of our folly. And they diverge a lot. Whether artistic, religious, sporting, or whatever, rituals and beliefs serve not so much to enlighten but to insulate the votary from waking up to the immediacy of life, from looking outside normal boundaries for better solutions. Prescribed behavior, detailed codes of conduct, unnatural environments, repetition of the expected—these all serve to protect the fearful adult child from the terrifying flames of freedom.

As an example, music can be powerfully transformative, but people often go to concerts and even the symphony—that holiest of holies—as a ritual: drinks first, nice clothes, chitchat in the lobby, clap now, "what piece is next," "let's go home." Just as in church, not much listening happens except in the hellfire segments. The Gita recognizes the feeling that once we catch the merest glimpse of the Absolute we want to retreat as fast as possible back to conventional images, in hopes that all our comfortable activities and attitudes will keep us safe. They don't. As Jung says, they keep us dead.

This ties in to the role of churches, governments, and the like as substitute parental figures. Their self-anointed task is to comfort us and relieve us of the anxiety of being fully human and alive. We are trained to keep the lid on everything, which makes us so much less than we could be! But being fearful children in our hearts, we will lash out at anyone who suggests lifting the lid; even nail them to a cross. We prefer to remain in darkness, even if we are secretly miserable and terrified, since it's familiar and bears the seal of approval. Odd isn't it?

In what I call my Expanding Boxes Theory, as we go through a life of creative exploration, we gradually expand our awareness. At certain moments we notice we are confined in a kind of psychological box, and as we continue to grow we fill it up. Like a chick inside an egg, we press harder and harder against our rigid container until it breaks open. For a time afterward we experience a soaring sense of relief and increased freedom, mixed with a measure of awe and fear, and undergo rapid expansion. But after a while we begin to notice that we are just in a bigger box, that there are still limits, and soon we will begin to confront our next set of constraints. I imagine the series of boxes goes on forever, so we should not mistake relative freedom for absolute liberation. And like a chick trying to crawl back inside its shattered egg, there is no going back to the previous box, except through a ridiculous charade of self-deception.

KRISHNA SAID,

BY MY FAVOR, ARJUNA, THIS
SUPREME FORM HAS BEEN SHOWN,
BY UNION WITH THE SELF, MADE
UP OF LIGHT, UNIVERSAL, ENDLESS,
PRIMAL, NEVER BEFORE SEEN BY ANY
OTHER THAN YOURSELF.

Krishna repeats the claim from verse 6 that what Arjuna has just been through is unique, never before seen by anyone. It sounds like he's saying that no one else is capable of attaining the same level of experience, but it would be absurd for the Gita to aver that only a single person—already dead in our own distant past—could attain a vision of the Absolute. That would imply there is no hope for any of us! What is actually meant is that while there is a general correspondence between every person's realization, its particular attributes are unique to the individual, and they are unique even each time an individual has such an experience. Since it is a baffling paradox that the universal must always come to our notice in a specific guise, we should take a close look at the implications of it.

First off, Arjuna's vision occurred by Krishna's favor. This means a guru or at least some type of additional assistance is an essential part of what has just taken place, what the Gita calls a vision of the supreme form. Soma itself is one kind of favor. Whatever the circumstances, the bipolar connection between seeker and sought achieves a far deeper intuitive realization than any linear thought process of an isolated individual, as has already been made eminently clear. We should remember that back in verses 3 and 4, Arjuna specifically requested a vision of the Absolute. His reaching out for knowledge is met by the guru's grace in supplying it, and the resulting fusion produces a superlative condition. This verse specifically states that the vision arises from yoga or union with the Self, that is, the union of a seeker with the universal ground of being, which often appears as a guru figure.

The string of lovely adjectives, "made up of light, universal, endless, primal," is as good a description of the indescribable as we can hope for. Light is the tissue of consciousness, and it fills all space (universal) and time (endless) as the primal One. This universal ground is integral to everyone. Therefore the last line of the verse must mean that Arjuna's vision is from his own unique perspective, and no one will see it exactly the way he did, yet it is available to everyone as their very nature. As it manifests, the Absolute is nonstatic, so its apparent form will be different from moment to moment. And no matter how pure the interpretation by an individual mind, it will inevitably be colored to a degree. In other words, every time someone has a vision of the Absolute it will be "never before seen," and by no one else. And as noted before, the vision will be shaped to a significant extent by the set and setting, by each person's frame of mind and local environmental factors. Every vision is a fabulous amalgam of temporal and eternal—individual and universal—elements.

The Gita's open-ended tolerance is a natural corollary of this kind of understanding. When you know the Absolute as the core of every being, you naturally love the good in them and have compassion for their shortcomings. You realize everyone's insight is absolutely unique, so there is no arbitrary division of "right" as opposed to "wrong" perspectives. We are all working to upgrade our understanding, and there is plenty of room for improvement everywhere. The only thing that really matters is to extricate ourselves from unwisdom and move toward wisdom, and the more support we offer each other, the more rapid the progress we will all make.

Interestingly, Einstein's relativity equations indicate that at the speed of light time is annulled. Since light fills the universe, a journey from one end to the other as light would take no time at all. It appears the ancient rishis were aware of this in their own way, long before the invention of modern ciphering.

NEITHER BY THE VEDAS, SACRIFICES,
NOR BY STUDY, NOR BY GIFTS, NOR BY
RITUAL, NOR BY SEVERE AUSTERITIES,
CAN I POSSIBLY BE SEEN IN SUCH A
FORM IN THE HUMAN WORLD, BY
ANYONE OTHER THAN YOU.

The Gita categorically denies the value of religion, any form of ritual activity, or any scheme whatever, in attaining the ultimate vision. There's nothing equivocal here at all. There is absolutely no way to plot a route to a goal in this business. The Absolute is far more mysterious than we can ever imagine. If conceived of as a goal it recedes indefinitely.

The inner and outer dialectics of yoga, conceived in a total context of the Absolute and applied in ever fresh ways to present circumstances, all guided and realized through bipolar interaction with a guru, which can be anything that brings enlightenment, pretty well sums up the Gita's recommendation for how to live. Those espousing formulas and systems, while they may be more or less admirable, fall outside the scope of wisdom in its highest conception.

It's virtually certain that no "ultimate" vision is possible. All are in some way limited, shaped by the perceiver. But any significant enlarging event—which is usually transmitted by a guru to a disciple, and just as usually inaccurately described as Ultimate—will flood our souls with light, called love, and we are transformed. The omnipresent quantum vacuum, as an example, has the energy of many nuclear explosions per cubic centimeter taking place continuously. Yet this is not something we perceive. We couldn't possibly handle that much power without damping it down with many layers of insulation. Still, we can know it is there mathematically, supporting the universe. Mental insulation, by the way, is called ignorance in Vedanta.

Our everyday visions can be compared to the integers, 1, 2, 3, and so on, while the Ultimate resembles infinity. Because it's so much bigger, the number 753 looks like infinity to a 3, even though it isn't. A 3 cannot possibly contain that large a number. But compared to infinity, 753 is essentially the same size as 3. However you conceive of infinity or the Absolute, the proof is in the pudding. If the ideation makes you more loving and wise, it is valuable. If it divides you from your fellows or causes confusion, it is false on some level.

We are welcome to have such transitory experiences as we are fortunate enough to encounter, but then we should move onward and upward. It is unhealthy to focus too much on any one partial vision, inevitably tainted with projections and fanciful imaginings. We are guided to cherish and honor them, then leave them behind so we can continue on our way. After all, we can't make the visions happen just by wishing; if we could that would be more evidence that they were only projections. A true mystic just opens their heart to the onrushing wave; they don't try to build a wave from spare parts lying around the house. A woman gives birth to a child, but she has no idea how to put one together from scratch. Something beyond us is at work here. We have only to relinquish our petty fixations to allow the Beyond to permeate our being with Truth, Beauty, and Goodness.

This is a perfect place to add some timeless words of wisdom from Lao Tzu. From the Tao Te Ching, verse 38, Gia-fu Feng's translation:

> *A truly good man is not aware of his goodness,*
> *And is therefore good.*

A foolish man tries to be good,
And is therefore not good.

A truly good man does nothing,
Yet leaves nothing undone.
A foolish man is always doing,
Yet much remains to be done.

When a truly kind man does something, he leaves nothing
*   undone.*
When a just man does something, he leaves a great deal to be
*   done.*
When a disciplinarian does something and no one responds,
He rolls up his sleeves in an attempt to enforce order.

Therefore when Tao is lost, there is goodness.
When goodness is lost, there is kindness.
When kindness is lost, there is justice.
When justice is lost, there is ritual.
Now ritual is the husk of faith and loyalty, the beginning of
*   confusion.*
Knowledge of the future is only a flowery trapping of Tao.
It is the beginning of folly.

Therefore the truly great man dwells on what is real and not
*   what is on the surface,*
On the fruit and not the flower.
Therefore accept the one and reject the other.[29]

BE NOT DISTRESSED, DO NOT BE CONFUSED, HAVING SEEN SUCH A TERRIBLE FORM OF MINE; FREE FROM FEAR, MENTALLY COMFORTED, AGAIN BEHOLD THAT VERY FORM OF MINE (PRESENTLY) HERE.

We can see from Krishna's words of consolation that Arjuna is distressed, confused, and fearful. The immediate aftereffect of an intense "trip" is often massive chaos, which can be very upsetting. The familiar categories and frameworks have been eradicated. It's like being returned temporarily to an infantile, preconceptual state. However it has been accessed, the state de-energizes the habitual persona, laden with defense mechanisms, leaving the seeker open and vulnerable. At this stage the guru may well act like a doting mother in comforting and caring for the recently reborn disciple.

When my guru Nitya Chaitanya Yati was staying with Ramana Maharshi, he had a mind-blowing experience induced by the Maharshi where he regressed to before he was born, and even before he was conceived. Afterward the normally impersonal Maharshi treated him with exceptional kindness, easing his reentry into the world. As Nitya tells it in his autobiography:

Eventually somebody tapped on my shoulder, and I came back to my senses. The Maharshi was no longer before me, and the people in the hall were also gone. Everyone had left for the dining hall. I was invited to come and eat. I walked as if in a dream. To my utter surprise, when I got to the dining hall I saw that the leaf [the banana leaf used as a food plate] on Maharshi's right hand was not claimed by anyone. I was asked to sit there. When food was served, Maharshi looked at my leaf as if to ascertain that every item served to him was also being given to me.[30]

Some modern psychotherapeutic techniques intentionally mimic birth to take the seeker to the very depths of their soul. It is generally true that the younger we are, the easier it is to effect changes in our neurochemistry. We tend to lose flexibility as we age, but this isn't an immutable law, as with Bob Dylan's line in the song "My Back Pages," "I was so much older then, I'm younger than that now." You can always evolve if you put your mind to it. But a little regression might facilitate the progression.

A stable mental orientation will redevelop at a rapid rate in a healthy psyche, but its new perspectives should be fresh and free of at least some of the glitches that plagued the old outlook. Then it is a true rebirth. The idea of being "born again" is used extremely loosely nowadays, but absent a soul-shattering experience like Arjuna's, it is merely a smug conceit, paying egotistical lip service to the real thing.

A pure experience of the Absolute transcends words and even the thoughts and concepts that are represented by words. It is invaluable to have a gentle program to help with "coming down" or "getting back to earth." Otherwise the aeronaut—temporarily perhaps a grinning idiot—is vulnerable to manipulation by people and events. When the One Beyond has been sighted, the bliss is so intense that everything is trusted to be beneficent. It's impossible to be critical during a time when there are no thoughts, as well as later on when every thought is immediately offset by its opposite in a global perspective. Moreover, it would be tragic to caution a person who is brimming with love to stop feeling it and guard themselves. They'll want to enjoy the sensation to the hilt. The guide's role at this time is to make sure there are no influences around that might fill the traveler's mind with poisonous ideas, because they will be very hard to dislodge once the bliss wears off.

The hippies launched into space by LSD in the 1960s became famous not so much for their insights and creativity as for their incoherence. Obviously the media always prefers to focus on failures rather than successes, but even so, not too many found meaningful interpretations of their experiences. In the conceptual vacuum and outright hostility they encountered, they cast about for whatever was close to hand. A fortunate few found teachers able to empathetically help shape their visions, and others banded together in communes for mutual support. But quite a few were lured into various religious sects, and many others worshipped the drugs themselves. Or they worshipped the musicians that accompanied the trips. Most of us clung to anything but an unadorned vision of truth. It seems that under social pressure we are doomed to make haste to clothe our idealistic visions in some kind of structure. Holding ten thousand suns worth of loving bliss in our hearts is just too intense, especially in a society that demands we suppress our light and be serious, so we can get a "useful" job.

It bears repeating that it's very important that Krishna does not grant Arjuna's request to appear in conventional religious guise. He goes directly back to being the ordinary friend and charioteer he has been all along. There is no exaggerated imagery being peddled, nothing that isn't universal. Arjuna's vision has its own meaning to him alone, and the less he repackages it in "standard issue" boxes, the greater its value will be. Krishna is just a normal guy, a regular human being, and he demonstrates for us just how amazing that is. And like him, we carry the Absolute in our very core. So when Krishna ignores Arjuna's plea, it's as though he is teasing him, saying, with a twinkle in his eye, "Wow, so I looked like Vishnu to you, eh? That's hilarious. What a trip!"

As noted earlier, Krishna's return to his ordinary human state also reflects the fact that in reality there is no going back to false ideals once they are seen for what they are. If innocence is lost it can never be fully regained. If you can't handle this, you shouldn't ask a guru—human or medicinal—to guide you to truth.

VERSE 50

SANJAYA SAID:
HAVING THUS SPOKEN TO ARJUNA,
KRISHNA AGAIN SHOWED HIS
OWN FORM, AND THE GREAT
SELF, BECOMING MILD IN FORM,
CONSOLED HIM WHO WAS
TERRIFIED.

The narrator returns briefly to add emphasis to this important moment. Krishna is once again seen as an ordinary mortal, who as a guru is soothing the newly rejuvenated disciple about to begin a fresh life. The apparent fierceness of his former state is counterbalanced now by a loving and nurturing one.

Many religions have sabotaged their own usefulness by portraying their central character as wholly different from everyone else. The very value of a saint or other "sacred" being is that they demonstrate what is possible for all people to achieve. Once they are perceived as being beyond imitation, the seeker must resign in despair, content to stand hat in hand as a beggar at the gate of the divine realm. The Vedanta of the Upanishads and the Gita maintains that each of us is the Absolute incarnate (such as in the teaching from the Chandogya Upanishad, *tat tvam asi,* "That thou art!") and our potential is infinite. We are not to wait for someone else to take steps for our betterment; we are the captains of our soul. So Krishna is just some regular fellow. Popular tales picturing him as a god are mostly later additions, or I should say subtractions. Actually, they are wonderful teaching stories, but they should not be mistaken for literal depictions.

Like Arjuna, all of us arrive at adult age in a state of shock. We are mentally and emotionally hampered by the traumas associated with changing our address from a womb to a battlefield. In response, many of us have the notion that if we can only control our inner turmoil and achieve a veneer of quietude, we will have reached the spiritual state.

Not at all. In most cases the "spiritual" technique initially adopted by a traumatized person is intended to suppress the inner turmoil with great effort, but like a pressure cooker the steam builds up until it bursts out through some psychological "relief valve." It is easy to go mad when this happens—or wind up in jail.

Socially acceptable outlets for the energy that we should direct toward our own enlightenment are nonpsychedelic drugs, entertainment, hard work, and the like. Basically, these are more distracting than enlightening, and with all the excellent entertainment available these days, it is possible to remain distracted for a whole lifetime.

By contrast, real spirituality shrugs off distractions to attend to a dynamic expression of our inner tendencies, along with a careful dousing of our excessive instinctual fires. In order to foster this, a guru will sometimes trick a disciple into losing control early in their relationship, so that any pent up energy is blown off and its traumatic origins stand revealed. Again, there is danger in this, because the guru or therapist can appear to be hostile, so the disciple may draw back, still highly charged with psychoses and neuroses. Freud's image is exactly right: although you have a terrible toothache, as the dentist approaches with his pliers to pull it out you can't help but push him away. Our self-protective instinct is that strong.

We must develop faith in the guru early on and anticipate being taught in the midst of extreme anguish part of the time. We would much prefer to retreat to a safe place where we could regain our mask of stability, but that would be to abandon the quest. Instead, we should redirect the energy released into a search of our soul.

The true spiritual calm comes only after weathering the challenges of many such storms. When we have been cured of our "toothaches" the guru will set aside the pliers and return to normal compassion and kindness.

This is the last of the string of extended or exalted verses in this chapter, signifying that the trip with its visions has now come to an end. Only a handful of these special verses remain in the Gita, all in chapter XV.

ARJUNA SAID:
BEHOLDING AGAIN THIS YOUR MILD HUMAN FORM, I AM NOW CALM, WITH MY MIND RESTORED TO ITS NATURAL STATE.

Arjuna has one final verse to reassure us that his trip is at last truly over and he feels like himself again. Sort of.

Calmed by his guru, things superficially appear as they once were, but they will never really be the same. As many an inner traveler has discovered, you can come back down afterward, but your relation to the world has been irrevocably changed. The experience is a kind of "brain boost" that imparts insights that cannot be completely ignored. New neural connections have been forged and old ones decommissioned. Orientation with the world is from a broadly enhanced perspective, and a hum of bliss and peacefulness persists long after the vision ends. The remainder of the Gita is aimed at reintegrating such an experience into normal life in the most salubrious manner. It will take all of the remaining seven chapters to lead Arjuna to the point that he can once again function optimally as an embodied being in a relativistic world. At the very end, though, he will receive his graduate diploma, with Krishna granting him his full freedom to make his own decisions.

Arjuna's vision is only one part of the whole story of his spiritual apprenticeship. A life suffused with the energy and insight of the Absolute is the yoga the Gita extols as the highest achievement of human endeavor. The horizontal and the vertical, actualities and ideals, are to be harmonized and integrated, not viewed in isolation as mutually exclusive. The world is not merely material or merely spiritual; it is both together. The full magnificence of the Gita's presentation cannot be adequately appreciated in words. We can only incline inwardly and be grateful to whatever fortunate process brought it to our attention, while resolving to take from it all the wisdom we can.

Having his mind restored to a natural state is essential for Arjuna's ongoing spiritual progress. He will have to be absolutely clearheaded to appreciate the high ideals Krishna will be showing him. One tragedy of the psychedelic era was that many people mistook the medium for the message, and they kept taking the drugs over and over, as if that were the key to enlightenment. The stress on the mind and body from such a regimen is too much, and many became burn-outs or misfits. The Gita is here reminding us of what all ancient societies knew very well: that these medicines are to be used sparingly to open the doors of perception, but not as a permanent place to hang out. We can learn much from them about who we are and where we are going, but then we still have to move toward enlightenment, in real life and not just in our fantasies.

One of the principal stumbling blocks to spiritual flowering is misunderstanding of the nature of reality. After an intense experience like Arjuna's, where our previously accepted core beliefs have been annulled, it is easy to become eccentric about the meaning of life. It takes time to regain a normal balance. In the immediate aftermath of a trip, two potential hazards loom large. While the well-guided disciple will be assisted to stay centered in neutrality, there is a temptation to either become megalomaniacal or its opposite, to dwell in utter self-abnegation. The shocked psyche either identifies with the entrancing vision and imagines itself as God, or it imagines an unbridgeable gap between it and God, which means it is nothing, a useless appendage. In fact, these poles are a dialectic, or the horns of a major dilemma, which must be resolved with a healthy synthesis of the two contrary ideas, neither of which is true by itself.

I've only met one or two obvious megalomaniacs in my life, and there is nothing to be done but to run away from them as fast as possible. But I know quite a number of the second type, the self-deprecators. I believe they are much more common, due to our drug-saturated and traumatized social environment, abetted by an education system designed to undermine individuality. Regardless, these friends have become fixated on the belief that everything is false, everything is meaningless, and they are worthless. In consequence, their lives have become dead-ended due to lack of any motivating value vision. Both types, the grandiose and the pusillanimous, can be extremely cynical because everybody they meet appears to be living a lie, while only they are holding to truth. Or maybe they feel that not even they are, so no one knows truth. This provides a negative ego reinforcement that is very difficult to get out from under, particularly since all outside advice is seen to be either hostile or foolish.

Arjuna is here assuring us that with the loving friendship of his guru, he has avoided this trap. He will wrestle with it philosophically in the next chapter, but he is holding fast to unity at the moment when it is most crucial, as he comes back to earth. I think we can safely predict an excellent outcome.

VERSE 52

KRISHNA SAID:
THIS FORM OF MINE WHICH YOU
HAVE SEEN IS VERY HARD TO SEE
INDEED; EVEN THE GODS EVER
ASPIRE TO BEHOLD THIS FORM.

Most of us have experienced powerful fear at some point in our life, and a very common response is to immerse ourselves in trivialities, the "hamster wheel" of life, in order to try to drive the fear out of our mind. Because of this, the social milieu consists of an endless series of tasks and pursuits to distract us from the fear of our demise. If you wanted to hide truth and keep it safe from discovery, this might well be the place to put it: right behind the fear. Then nearly everything we did would lead us away from where we most needed to look.

Verse 15 of the Isha Upanishad reads: "The entrance to Truth is closed with a golden disc. That, you, Oh Nourisher, open (so that I), established in Truth and Law, may see."[31] The metaphor is that the sun—the Source of all life—is hidden directly behind a sun-like image. This is by far the best place to hide the sun, and it is at the same time a perfect symbol of how our minds substitute conceptions for reality. We become enamored with ideas in themselves and stop searching for what they refer to. No wonder the vision of truth is so rare!

It is amusing that "the gods ever aspire" to have these visions also, which reminds us that they are partial beings just as we are. In ancient times in India the moon was poetically imagined to be a barrel of soma juice. The waning of the moon indicated that the gods were drinking the soma, which is their favorite beverage. After they polished it off, it would be replenished while they were recovering from their intoxication. We like to imagine that gods are all-wise, yet apparently they enjoy getting a good cosmic buzz on, just as we do.

And as we well know, the soma juice itself is to be drunk by whosoever is moved to catch a glimpse of the elusive form of the Absolute, with its infinite varieties of expression.

NOT BY WORSHIP, NOR BY AUSTERITY, NOR BY GIFTS, NOR BY SACRIFICE, CAN I BE SEEN IN THIS FORM AS YOU HAVE SEEN ME.

Verse 48 is repeated for emphasis and to set up the final declaration in the following verse. Krishna has to say it twice, because this idea is resisted with all the might and main of the many vested interests that peddle salvation. Not by doing anything other than entering into the Absolute does one attain the Absolute. All steps on the path are merely steps on paths, valid in their own right, for exactly what they are, but not leading anywhere beyond themselves. This is a key tenet of Advaita Vedanta, or nondualism.

All four of these categories of futile striving—worship, austerity, gift giving, and sacrifice—can be lumped together under the title "proper religious behavior." As seekers we want to know what we should *do,* what the right activity for us is. Many religions purvey the idea that by being good and doing what we are told to do, we will obtain admission to heaven or some similar exalted state hereafter. Krishna is unequivocal that whatever the benefit of being good—and it is certainly favorable for living in the world—it doesn't bring the vision of the Absolute.

Most religious folk are very fond of their embroidered imaginative heaven-worlds, and they find a way to color even the spare and scientific Gita with exotic notions that are quite foreign to it. In case Arjuna has such tendencies, Krishna gives him a second chance to grasp the baldly stated case that the Absolute is beyond all programs. While religion is tolerated as appropriate for some, and good as far as it goes, that doesn't mean it is actually efficacious for attaining the highest. Narayana Guru famously said that whatever a man's religion, it was good insofar as it made him a better person. Period.

Toward the end of the Gita all these categories will be thoroughly assessed, and Krishna will assert that they should not be given up. At their best they are a fine, healthy way to live. But attaining the Absolute requires us to go beyond mechanical activities to tap into something that remains mysterious, no matter how hard we try to grasp it.

At the peak of the psychedelic movement of the 1960s a belief caught on that every form of conditioning and behavior should be discarded and that doing so would transform people into divine beings who were no longer bound by necessity. It was a wonderful fantasy, but there is as yet no evidence for it being true. We inhabit bodies and minds that require sustenance and maintenance, and we ignore our needs at our peril. Many who took that idea to extremes were unable to ever find their balance again, becoming unmoored souls wandering through life like hungry ghosts. What was missing for them was sane guidance from a wise helper or even a book like the Gita, in which great pains are taken to restore its readers to a fully functioning status.

So, while it is true that no formal ritual by itself produces unity with the Beyond, some intelligently conceived activity is essential for our mental and physical health. Just because it doesn't get you high is no reason to throw it away. Your brothers and sisters—indeed all creatures—need you to be there for them, and you need to be there for yourself, too.

It is of more than passing interest that soma ingestion is not included in this verse's list of ineffective actions, however. It may well be that a psychedelic vision is indeed what chapter XI describes for us, and if so, Krishna's caveat applies to it also. Soma provides a vision, an image of the Absolute, but continuing to take it after you have learned its lessons is a waste of time and will keep you stuck in a dream world.

Psychedelic experimentation can at least provide beginner training in one-pointed devotion, which the next two verses spell out as the way that really does work. When all is said and done, in the impossible tautology of spiritual realization, you become the Absolute just by being it.

BUT BY DEVOTION THAT EXCLUDES ALL ELSE I CAN BE KNOWN, AND IN PRINCIPLE ENTERED INTO.

"Devotion that excludes all else" could also be called absorption or one-pointed attention. Krishna is speaking here of a perfect bipolarity between the Absolute and the devotee; anything tacked on by way of conditioned imagery can only detract from the direct reciprocal relationship. Regarding full-fledged devotion Nataraja Guru says, "There is always implied in such instances an identity or unity of a very thorough character as between the seeker and the wisdom of the Absolute. Such references by no means suggest the weak variety of *bhakti* (devotion), which mostly consists of clashing cymbals, bell-ringings, and parrot-like muttering of *mantrams* (sacred syllables). But of course such practices have their justification, in so far as they displace worse practices!"[32]

There are two directions to the devotion Krishna counsels here. One is the straightforward dedication to the principle of the Absolute itself. The other is an ongoing effort to exclude extraneous factors. If we can shrug off all trivial imagery as it arises, it will allow us to occasionally take a peek behind the golden disc blocking truth. This does not mean we should avoid *all* imagery though, only that which is irrelevant to our development.

The weakness of worshipful forms of devotion is that they are aimed at fixed mental images such as rigidly conceived gods. The Absolute is an ever-living reality, access to which is blocked by all such conceptions.

The Gita presents yoga, the uniting of opposites, as an unadorned and nonstatic method of bipolarity with the ever-new Absolute.

In a similar analogy, Narayana Guru, in verse 9 of his *One Hundred Verses of Self-Instruction,* proffers the image of a contemplative sitting in meditation under a tree in the jungle. Clinging vines are growing up the tree, and these reach out and try to ensnare the yogi, but he is ever alert and keeps himself free of their clutches. So there is a twofold effort involved: contemplative devotion to the Absolute and a simultaneous devotion to avoiding entanglements.

Flipping through my stack of Gita translations, Nataraja Guru's is the only one that reads "in principle entered into." The rest say simply "entered into." The word *tattvena* (meaning "in principle") is ignored. Since the Absolute is always here, we are already in it and so entering from outside is impossible. Entering "in principle" acquiesces to this fact. *Tattvena* also means "truly" or "in truth," which does find its way into some of the translations. A veiled meaning comes in reference to *tat tvam* (*asi*), That thou (art). Only when you realize you *are* the Absolute have you fully entered the Absolute.

Devotion is also the subject of the next chapter of the Gita, which follows immediately on the heels of Arjuna's vision. The two last verses of this chapter provide an artful transition, as well as an assertion of just how crucial enlightened devotion to truth is.

VERSE 55

HE WHO DOES ACTIONS THAT ARE MINE, WHOSE SUPREME IS MYSELF, WHOSE DEVOTION IS TO ME, DEVOID OF ATTACHMENT, FREE FROM ENMITY TO ALL BEINGS—HE REACHES ME, ARJUNA.

Any time you think "I am doing this because . . ." or even more subtly, "I am doing this," an element of duality is injected into the activity. While this is perfectly fine in ordinary circumstances, the Gita advocates the artistic—sometimes called spiritual—temperament, where unitive action is essential. The musician, dancer, meditator, or tripper doesn't have time to stop and think dualistic thoughts. They are intrusive and disrupt the flow. Adequate preparations having been made, artists must dive with their whole being into what is being performed. Only then will they be able to express real expertise.

Keeping in mind that in the Gita "Me" and "Mine" refer to the Absolute, we can retranslate this verse as follows:

> *The one who does Absolutist actions, in other words, who*
> *performs unitive activity* [as instructed in chapters
> II–V];

Whose philosophical orientation is centered around the
harmonizing factor of the Absolute;
Who can attune completely with the Absolute and not
become bogged down by irrelevancies;
Who is free to go psychologically wherever the winds of the
Absolute might blow them;
And who sees the Absolute in all beings, therefore becoming
surpassingly kind;
This is the model devotee who attains the Absolute.

EPILOGUE

In his mind's eye, Arjuna finds himself far from the battlefield. As the predawn hush of the surrounding jungle gives way to the thrum of the awakening day and the magenta blush of the sky fades toward the deepest blue, the longest night of his life comes to a gentle close. The newfound harmony of his soul is his only covering as he reclines on the warm ground, his mind alternately flashing and soaring high on the wings of fresh insights. His body surges with bliss and a serene calm permeates his whole being, still vibrating with the celestial images that so recently poured through him. He barely notices as Krishna slips off toward the simple hut that serves as his recondite ashram.

This has been the most amazing and revealing day Arjuna has ever experienced, and he still cannot quite believe his good fortune. His confusion and reluctance to pursue the course of his prescribed destiny led him straight into the arms of a great teacher, who miraculously raised him up from his conflicted state as if from a tomb. Gratitude for his new lease on life surges through him. It simply cannot be an accident that the universe is so kind as to offer him succor at exactly the crucial moment!

Exhausted but elated, Arjuna feels his psyche start to calm down. He begins to be aware of the lumps of sand and blades of grass under him. For a moment he drops off, but then he jerks awake, reluctant to let go of his profound peacefulness.

But he is too tired. After a brief rest, there will be so much to attend to, so much to learn! He is quivering with eagerness to dive in to the challenges life has spread before him like a ceremonial banquet. He isn't sure what Krishna still wants to teach him, but he can't wait to find out. His old attitudes no longer mean anything to him other than bondage. He has so much new territory to explore, more than he ever imagined, and the thought thrills him to the core. Smiling the barest whisper of a smile, Arjuna gently subsides into a dreamless sleep.

NOTES

1. My website, Nitya Teachings, can be accessed at http://scottteitsworth .tripod.com.
2. Kingsolver, *The Lacuna,* 151.
3. Merton, *The New Man,* 13.
4. Doblin, "Letter," 2.
5. Aurobindo, *Bhagavad Gita and Its Message,* 174–75.
6. Daumal, *Mount Analogue,* 150–51.
7. Yati, *That Alone,* 242.
8. Bateson and Bateson, *Angels Fear,* 136.
9. Taylor, *My Stroke of Insight,* 30–31.
10. Wasson, Ruck, and Hofmann, *The Road to Eleusis,* 19.
11. Doblin, "Pahnke's 'Good Friday Experiment'," 1–28.
12. Keohane, "How Facts Backfire."
13. Gopnik, "How Babies Think," 81.
14. Jung, "The Stages of Life," 392–93.
15. Merton, *The New Man,* 9–10.
16. Nataraja, *The Bhagavad Gita,* 488.
17. Bird and Sherwin, *American Prometheus,* 309.
18. Aurobindo, *Bhagavad Gita and Its Message,* 181.
19. Nataraja, *The Bhagavad Gita,* 496.
20. Taylor, *My Stroke of Insight,* 147.
21. Guarneri, *The Heart Speaks,* 155 ff.
22. Twain, *Letters from the Earth,* 212–13.
23. Yati, *Love and Blessings,* 350.
24. Stafford, from "A Ritual to Read to Each Other," 75–76.

25. Dnyaneshwar, *Gita Explained,* 157–58.

26. Monier-Williams, *A Sanskrit-English Dictionary,* s.v. *aprameya* and *prameya.*

27. Yati, "*Svanubhavagiti Satakam,* Aesthetics and Transcendence," 7. A translation with a different numbering system by Muni Narayana Prasad is also listed in the bibliography.

28. Jung, *Memories, Dreams, Reflections,* 297.

29. Lao Tzu, *Tao Te Ching,* v. 38.

30. Yati, *Love and Blessings,* 142.

31. Narayana Gurukula, comp., *Dhyana Manjusha,* 20.

32. Nataraja, *The Bhagavad Gita,* 508.

BIBLIOGRAPHY

Aurobindo, Sri. *Bhagavad Gita and Its Message*. Twin Lakes, Wis.: Lotus Press, 1995.

———. *Essays on the Gita*. New York: The Sri Aurobindo Library, 1950.

Bateson, Gregory, and Mary Catherine Bateson. *Angels Fear: Towards an Epistemology of the Sacred*. Toronto: Bantam Books, 1987.

Bird, Kai, and Martin J. Sherwin. *American Prometheus: The Triumph and Tragedy of J. Robert Oppenheimer*. New York: Vintage Books, 2006.

Crawford, O. G. S. *The Eye Goddess*. London: Phoenix House, 1957.

Daumal, Rene. *Mount Analogue*. New York: Pantheon Books, 1960.

Doblin, Rick. "Letter from Rick Doblin, Ph.D." *MAPS Bulletin* XIX, no. 1 (Summer 2009): 2.

———. "Pahnke's 'Good Friday Experiment': A Long-Term Follow-Up and Methodological Critique." *The Journal of Transpersonal Psychology* 23, no. 1 (1991).

Dnyaneshwar, Maharaj. *Gita Explained*. Translated by Manu Subedar. 3rd ed. Bombay: Kodak House, 1945.

Easwaran, Eknath. *Like a Thousand Suns*. Petaluma, Calif.: Nilgiri Press, 1979.

Gopnik, Alison. "How Babies Think." *Scientific American* (July 2010): 76–81.

Grof, Stanislav, M.D. *LSD Psychotherapy*. 3rd ed. Sarasota, Fla.: Multidisciplinary Association for Psychedelic Studies, 2001.

Guarneri, Mimi. *The Heart Speaks*. New York: Touchstone, 2006.

Hume, Robert Ernest. *The Thirteen Principal Upanishads*. 2nd ed. London: Oxford University Press, 1931.

Huxley, Aldous. *The Doors of Perception and Heaven and Hell*. New York: Harper & Row, 1963.

Jung, C. G. *Memories, Dreams, Reflections.* Final rev. ed. New York: Pantheon Books, 1973.

———. "The Stages of Life." In Complete Works 8: *The Structure and Dynamics of the Psyche.* 2nd ed. Princeton, N.J.: Princeton University Press, 1969.

Keohane, Joe. "How Facts Backfire." *Boston Globe,* 11 July 2010.

Kingsolver, Barbara. *The Lacuna.* New York: HarperCollins, 2009.

Lao Tzu. *Tao Te Ching.* Translated by Gia-fu Feng. New York: Vintage Books, 1972.

Merton, Thomas. *The New Man.* New York: The New American Library, 1963.

Miller, Alice. *For Your Own Good: Hidden Cruelty in Child-Rearing and the Roots of Violence.* 3rd ed. New York: Farrar Straus and Giroux, 1990.

Monier-Williams, Sir Monier. *A Sanskrit-English Dictionary.* 1970 ed. London: Oxford University Press, 1899.

Narayana, Guru. *Atmopadesa Satakam: One Hundred Verses of Self-Instruction.* See Nitya Chaitanya Yati, *That Alone,* below.

Narayana Gurukula, comp. *Dhyana Manjusha.* Varkala, South India: Mangala Press, n.d.

Nataraja, Guru. *The Bhagavad Gita: A Sublime Hymn of Dialectics.* 2nd ed. New Delhi: D.K. Printworld, 2008.

———. *Dialectics.* 3rd ed. New Delhi: D.K. Printworld, 2010.

———. *Unitive Philosophy.* New Delhi: D.K. Printworld, 2005.

———. *Wisdom: The Absolute Is Adorable.* New Delhi: D.K. Printworld, 1995.

Prasad, Muni Narayana. *Narayana Guru Complete Works.* New Delhi: National Book Trust, India, 2006.

Radhakrishnan, S., trans. *The Bhagavadgita.* New York: Harper & Row, 1973.

Stafford, William. "A Ritual to Read to Each Other." In *The Way It Is: New and Selected Poems.* St. Paul: Graywolf Press, 1998.

Stevens, Jay. *Storming Heaven: LSD and the American Dream.* New York: The Atlantic Monthly Press, 1987.

Taylor, Jill Bolte. *My Stroke of Insight.* New York: Viking, 2006.

Twain, Mark. *Letters from the Earth.* New York: Harper & Row, 1962.

Wasson, R. Gordon, Carl A. P. Ruck, and Albert Hofmann. *The Road to Eleusis.* New York: Harvest/HBJ, 1978.

Williams, George M. *Handbook of Hindu Mythology.* New York: Oxford University Press, 2003.

Yati, Nitya Chaitanya. *The Bhagavad Gita: A Sublime Hymn of Yoga Composed by the Ancient Seer Vyasa.* 2nd ed. New Delhi: D.K. Printworld, 1993.

————. *Love and Blessings: The Autobiography of Guru Nitya Chaitanya Yati.* 1st American ed. Portland, Ore.: Narayana Gurukula, 2003.

————. *Meditations on the Self.* 2nd ed. Portland, Ore.: Narayana Gurukula, 2005.

————. *Narayana Guru.* New Delhi: Indian Council of Philosophical Research, 2005.

————. "*Svanubhavagiti Satakam,* Experiential Aesthetics and Imperiential Transcendence." *Gurukulam* V (First Quarter, 1989); and *Gurukulam* VIII (First Quarter, 1992).

————. *That Alone: The Core of Wisdom.* New Delhi: D.K. Printworld, 2003.

INDEX